AF379378

Eternal Unfolding

A JOURNEY THAT TURNED INTO
A DIFFERENT KIND OF
LOVE STORY

RICHARD P. FONTANIE

Eternal Unfolding:
A Journey that turned into a different
kind of love story
Copyright © 2019 by Richard P. Fontanie

All rights reserved. No part of this publication may
be reproduced, distributed, or transmitted in any
form or by any means, including photocopying,
recording, or other electronic or mechanical
methods, without the prior written permission of
the author, except in the case of brief quotations
embodied in critical reviews and certain other
non-commercial uses permitted by copyright law.

Unless otherwise indicated, all Scripture
quotations re taken from THE HOLY BIBLE, NEW
INTERNATIONAL VERSION®NIV® Copyright
© 1973,1978,1984,2011 by Biblica, Inc.® Used by
permission. All rights reserved worldwide.

All other quotes, verses and poems are drawn from
the public domain.

Tellwell Talent
www.tellwell.ca

ISBN
978-0-2288-0307-2 (Paperback)
978-0-2288-0308-9 (eBook)

Table of Contents

Dedication

To my wonderful family
with enduring love:
my wife
Carolyn,
our daughters
Treena and Leanne,
their husbands
Dale and David,
our grandchildren
Julia, Leo and Charlie.
Without them, I wouldn't have imagined
Julech and Catrela Daldavie.

Preface

THE IDEA FOR WRITING A BOOK OF THIS NATURE CAME TO ME AS
I was preparing an article about life's purpose as a reflection
of love. It is a fictional story of a character, Julech Daldavie,
who experiences a spiritual awakening as he hikes among the
mountains surrounding Fernie, B.C. The characters and story
line jumped from my imagination as I put pen to paper or more
correctly, fingers on the computer keyboard.

Although the story line in *Eternal Unfolding* is fictional you
may find Julech's meditations and reflections cause you to
reflect on your own spiritual journey.

All main characters within the story are imaginary and
are not intended to represent any known living or dead individuals. Others, who are quoted or mentioned such as Pope
Francis (1936-), Mother Teresa (1910-1997), Corrie ten Boom
(1892-1983), Francis of Assisi (1181-1226), and Teresa of Avila
(1515-1582) are well known and found in the public domain.

Fernie BC, Nelson, BC, and all the rivers and mountains
mentioned exist. The animal and bird behavior as described
are accurate as far as I am aware, except of course for Chippy
who cannot converse in human language.

Fernie is a bustling year-round resort community, located in the south eastern part of British Columbia, Canada. Although Fernie is referred to as a town it is a city which was incorporated in 1904. It's current permanent population is approximately 4200 with another 2300 part-time residents swelling its numbers during peak recreational seasons.

There are numerous hiking trails into the mountains and backwoods around Fernie but the trail and its formation Julech traveled are invented. The trail is reminiscent of the trail joining Lakehead, Heiko, and the Hartley Lake Road. That trail can be hiked in one or two days rather than the 12 days described in the story. Julech's hike twisted and turned, went off on side trails that may or may not exist. The first lake may resemble Island Lake, the second lake at the junction of Mount Fernie and the Three Sisters as well as the glacier on the Three Sisters may not exist. The third lake may resemble Hartely Lake. I haven't hiked the Heiko Trail or other trails mentioned except in my imagination. However, the findings and stories told along the way are mostly true. The legends described in the story are long standing tales told and retold among Fernie folk and recorded in chronicles about Fernie.

You will find that *Eternal Unfolding* follows a Christian theme, however, I hope its content will appeal to all people of good will embracing both non-believers and those from other faith communities.

Thank you for reading,
Richard P. Fontanie

Created from Love

"To be fully alive we search for
the meaning of life and
contribute to the
well-being of others by
pursuing the qualities of love,
forgiveness, mercy and goodness."
Julech

The Journey Begins
~ Love's Image

IT WAS A GORGEOUS JULY MORNING, NOT A CLOUD IN SIGHT AND the temperature was just right for hiking. This part of the trail was dusty and well-travelled. It snaked up the mountain side and gave a clear view of the valley below. Julech Daldavie was struck with how far the valley stretched. He thought he could see where Alberta and British Columbia joined at the Crowsnest Pass.

He was on a path following the base of Lizard Range. He stopped and looked back. He absorbed the panoramic view of the mountains that surrounded Fernie BC. He easily picked out the mountains called the Three Sisters, Proctor, Hosmer, Castle and the Fernie Ridge.

He had been hiking for about two hours when he looked up at the clear blue sky and shouted out loud, "God, or whatever or whoever, are you up there?"

There was no answer.

He wandered a little further and peered down into the valley.

"Are you, whoever you are, down there?"

As he expected there was no answer, just the echo of his voice.

Julech had walked for at least an hour when another hiker came into view. He was short, stocky and muscular. He looked a little older than Julech, sported a well-kept greying beard, walked with a staff for balance and was clothed in well-worn hiking gear. It appeared that he had been hiking for a few days. Julech wondered whether he had scaled the Lizard Range and was on his way back to the Lodge below.

When they met, the hiker said, "It's a great day for hiking." He paused then asked, "How far up the trail are you going?"

"I'm not sure. I'm just following it and trying to take in all the beauty around me."

"Is that all?"

"Not really. I'm searching for something that I can't really explain. The only thing I can come up with is that there must be more to life than what I experience on a daily basis."

"That's heavy stuff," said the hiker, as he began to resume his downward hike. He went about 15 meters then looked over his shoulder and called out to Julech, "Open your eyes and ears. Look and listen deeper."

The hiker quickly fell from sight.

"What the heck does that mean. I can see the beauty around me, I told him that. I can hear the wind, the trees rustle, and the birds flying overhead. Look and listen deeper?" Julech said to himself.

Julech looked up the trail. He couldn't see where it was going. All he could see was another bend ahead and more trees. He never scoped out the trail before he left. He could have checked it out on his GPS device or at the cabin located at the start of the climb. But he didn't. His friends told him that the trail was lengthy, winding and scenic. It would take him twelve days to complete if he hiked 15 to 20 kilometres a day.

The trail formed a loop. It followed the Lizard Range, went around the back of the Fernie Ridge, Three Sisters and Mount Proctor, meandered in front of Mount Hosmer and then circled back to Fernie paralleling the highway.

The start of the path on the west side of the town was first traveled by deer. They would amble up the mountain side, munch on the grass and leaves and ended up at a lake about 50 kilometres from their starting point. There the deer grazed on the tall grass and loafed around in the lake.

The path was further beaten into shape by Indigenous hunters as they stalked the deer for needed meat and hides. During the latter part of the 19th century prospectors found the trail and pushed it even further until it formed the existing loop. The prospectors were looking for "black gold" or coal. They had learned that coal was somewhere in the Crowsnest mountains, but they didn't find it on the loop.

Over time, tall grass and brush buried parts of the trail. During the 1930s economic depression the government hired unemployed men to reopen it.

People came from all parts of the world to challenge both their skill and endurance on the trail. It was time Julech tested it.

He wanted to make sure he had sufficient supplies to last the 12 days. He had made a supply list and posted it on a shelf in his basement. His backpack could hold 25 kilos of supplies and gear. Every time he added an item to his pack he ticked it off his list.

He packed dried food supplies, protein bars, peanut butter and honey mix, matches two pieces of flint, fish hooks and line, snare wire, collapsible cooking ware, a backwoods stove and isobutane canister, a first aid kit and a noise maker, a few toiletries and zip lock bags, water purifier tabs, dysentery pills (just in case), deep woods bug repellent, sun screen, rain suit and wind jacket, a canister of water, a tarp, 8x10 clear plastic, an ultra-thin tent, a Swiss Army Knife, and a micro bivy-bag.

All in all, the backpack weighed 15 kilos according to the scale he had rigged up. He was happy with that because he had learned from a hiking journal that the average weight for this type of hike was 20 kilos. He felt he could hike with 15 kilos on his back with ease.

His first inclination was to leave his smartphone at home. On second thought he said to himself, "My phone has a camera, flashlight, several downloaded books, music and access to a 911 number in case of emergency. I better take it."

He turned off his e-mail, stuffed the phone into his side pocket and placed an extra solar powered battery into his backpack.

Before leaving, he checked the weather forecast. Much to his liking it was going to be a warm and sunny July.

"Are you sure you want to do this?" Catrela asked.

Catrela was his beloved soul partner but in no way was she going on this journey. She loved Julech, but this was his venture, not hers.

"Yes. We've been talking about this hike for several months and now I'm ready."

Julech had planned this hike as a way to escape from his daily grind, do some soul searching, and rejuvenate before he had to start his next project.

He was a business consultant and had just finished a major project that required laser-like focus, engagement with over twenty business people, and the management of a team of twelve. He had to deal with hundreds of emails a day, combined with telephone calls from his project team and business associates. Since he was the lead for the project he received those emails and calls at all hours of the day and night. He was burnt out and needed a quiet break where he could unplug and be unavailable.

Catrela drove her husband in their old sliver Ford SUV to the Lodge where the trail began. She was concerned about her husband but knew he was an experienced hiker and would be able to take care of himself.

The Lodge was at the bottom of a ski hill. It was a large four-story stone-faced facility that housed over 100 guests at the peak of the skiing season. It had two lounges, three outdoor hot tubs and a café.

Catrela and Julech headed for the café where a hand full of vacationers were eating breakfast. They each ordered a cup of cappuccino.

They nursed their coffee in silence. They were both thinking of the hike ahead. He, looking forward to the journey. She, anxiously awaiting his return.

After what seemed like a long time but in reality, was only about 30 minutes, they stood up, and right there in the middle of the coffee shop they hugged, kissed and exchanged one more "I love you." Then they headed out to the SUV.

Julech wore a pair of convertible khaki pants. The kind that allowed him to zip off the bottom half of the legs. He had on a light T shirt, his favorite hiking boots and a *Chapeau*, affectionately called the "Hat". He strapped a hunting knife to his belt and picked up his hiking stick that his neighbor had carved for him. He lifted his backpack onto his shoulders and after one more kiss and "I love you," he took his first steps toward the mountain trail.

Catrela watched as Julech waved to her and then he disappeared among the trees.

Julech wondered if this venture of his was too much of a selfish act as Catrela and he always travelled together. They had long discussion about the hike, potential dangers and their 12-day separation. Catrela assured him that she was ok with it.

"You enjoy hiking, and I don't," she said. "Besides I will keep myself busy tending to our garden and my flowers. Don't be silly. Go, I'll be fine."

Still, Julech wondered whether she said that to please him or did she really mean it?

It seemed he had walked only a short time when he met that first hiker.

"Look and listen deeper," he repeated the bearded hiker's shout-out.

Julech kept walking along the trail. He listened to the songs of the birds. He heard the dee-dee of a chickadee. He watched a robin, struggle to get a worm out of the rocky ground for her little ones chirping up in a tree a few meters away. In the distance he heard the irritating caw of crows and hoped they didn't have an eye on the robin's chicks. He saw a bluebird sitting on an old stump singing a delicate love song to his mate. He was struck by the bluebird's bright turquoise feathers against the background of brown rotting wood.

"What an awesome color," he whispered.

He quietly pulled out his phone to take a picture, but the bluebird fluttered away before he could set and position the camera.

"Dang! Too noisy." He replaced the phone back into his pocket.

The smells of the clean air and the evergreens on each side of the trail reminded him of his youth. He had grown up in a small town surrounded by mountains just like the one where he now lived. He and his friends had often climbed the side of those mountains to pick blueberries or just to have a fun-filled outing.

He always brought his trusty Brownie Kodak camera on those jaunts and took pictures of anything that struck him as unusual. Back then he was careful not to take too many pictures as he had to leave the film at Kasper's Camera Shop and wait a week before it was developed.

"Times have sure changed," he said to himself. "Today we can view, click and save a picture instantly on our smartphone cameras."

One of his favorite hikes was along the banks of the Elk river. He would spend whole days walking up and down those banks looking for a quiet place to fish and after finding one he would mark it in a little book he kept in his back pocket. He called it his *Fishing Book.* He didn't want to forget those spots. Later he would return to them with his fishing gear to test his skill against the rainbow trout.

He smiled as he remembered how often the fish out-smarted him and then laughed out loud as he said, "I gotcha this time."

Julech looked around sheepishly. There was no one there to hear him.

The sun had edged closer to the middle of the sky and the temperature had warmed up considerably since he had left the lodge. Little rivulets of perspiration rolled from his brow and the backpack straps dug into his shoulders. It was time to take a break.

He approached a clearing with a small stream trickling down the mountain side. There was a log positioned so that it overlooked the valley and a circle of rocks next to it. It looked like a place where other hikers had lit a fire. Perhaps it was a resting place where people stopped for lunch.

He shrugged off his backpack, loosened his boots and sat on the log.

He had been sitting for about fifteen minutes when it dawned on him that this was the first time that he had sat down since he had left Catrela three hours ago. It felt good.

When he took off his backpack he could almost hear his shoulders say, "Thanks' buddy, it's about time!" And his feet tingled a song of relief.

He peered into the valley.,

"I'm just getting started and already my shoulders and feet are complaining."

Somehow, they seemed to respond, "We're not complaining, we just needed a break. Most days you sit in an office. We're not use to such heavy work. We'll be ready to go again in about an hour."

He pulled out a sandwich, some dried fruit and nuts, and his water canister. He was pleased that he had prepared a sandwich for lunch but hadn't planned a lunch menu for the following days.

"Oh well, tomorrow will take care of itself. Let me enjoy what I have today," he said with his mouthful.

He moved from the log to sit by the little stream and under a canopy of trees. He could still see the valley below and the expansive sky.

He looked over the valley and blue sky and mused, "It can't get better than this. Maybe I should stay here and forget the rest of the trip."

That was a different take on the questions he asked earlier that day, "Are you up there?" and "Are you down there?" Now he speculated, "It can't get any better than this." Again, the bearded hiker's comment about "look and listen deeper" crossed his mind.

A few clouds formed and peppered the sky. It was still warm, but the clouds provided some relief from the hot sun. He replenished his water canister, tightened up his laces and slipped on the backpack. He wanted to take advantage of the clouds.

Julech returned to his thoughts about hiking.

Several years ago, he had attended a three-week retreat at a Benedictine Monastery called The Abbey, built high on a ridge overlooking a bountiful valley. Every day, the retreatants walked up and down a gravel road that led to the Monastery. They along with Father Alphonsus, a deeply religious man and a philosophy professor, explored the teachings of the classical philosophers like Aristotle and Plato. Father Alphonsus would throw out a question and let the retreatants explore possible answers. He would say, "Draw from your experience and studies, but think for yourself."

"Good old Father Alphonsus. I'm going to use that bit of advice during this hike."

He remembered how much he had enjoyed exploring the 80 hectares of land around the Monastery. It seemed that the little trails which weaved in and out of the grounds were endless. He recalled that one of the trails took him three kilometres to the community below the Monastery. That was a fair walk. It pushed through thickets and shrubs that sprinkled a path along a ridge. At one point he was able to see the expansive Frazer Valley with its lush green gardens, lakes and endless roads.

Julech loved those trails. He followed them almost daily. The walks were peaceful yet at the same time invigorating. His favorite time for walking was around 4:30 in the afternoon when the monks were chanting *Vespers*.

Mid-way through the retreat the retreatants would venture out on an all-day hike. The hike was about 30 kilometres long and wound around a lake and up the mountain opposite the Monastery. They would leave about 8:30 in the morning and return in time for Vespers at 4:30 in the afternoon. To hike that distance in that short of time meant they had to hustle. They usually returned with a few blisters on their feet and sore muscles in their legs. Julech later learned that hiking mid-retreat was a way for retreatants to regroup after a period of intensive self-reflection.

He remembered another hiking experience when he had led 13 to 15-year-old Boy Scouts to the Kokanee Glaciers located near Nelson, BC. This was a bit of taxing hike for those young fellows because over a weekend they had to hike from their base camp near the Kootenay lake, climb up the Kokanee trail, sleep under the stars, scale the Kokanee Mountain to reach the glaciers, and return to base camp. Those hikes were always a camping highlight and a character builder for the boys.

"You know Julech," he said to himself, "Catrela was right, I do enjoy hiking."

It was now approaching three o'clock. He had been on the trail for almost six hours and his legs were beginning to cramp. It was time to look for a spot for the night.

Around the next bend he came across a clearing on the side of the trail. It was lined with spruce trees and filled with lush green grass sprinkled with buttercups and firewood blossoms. There was a pool of water, fed by a sparkling stream.

"Just what the doctor ordered," he thought.

He slipped off his backpack and stepped out of his boots.

"Thank you," his shoulders and feet said.

He inspected his feet. "Thank goodness I don't have any blisters."

Julech flopped down on the cool grass and looked up into the sky.

"Are you up there or are you down here?"

The fresh air and the climb had tuckered him out. He was dog tired. He learned a long time ago that when he was tired from working hard he needed to catch some shut eye. Usually after a ten minute power nap he would wake up refreshed and ready to tackle his next task. This time was no different, however it wasn't brain fatigue he felt, but bone and muscle fatigue.

Jake saw a body laying on the grass.

It wasn't moving.

"Is he dead or alive?"

He silently crept up to it, looked down and watched for signs of movement. He was relieved when he saw the body's chest slowly and rhythmically breathe in and out. However, he wasn't sure if the guy was alright.

He gave him a light jab with his boot.

Julech woke up with a start. He wasn't a fighter by any means, but he jumped up awkwardly and put out his fists.

"Hold on there!" Jake exclaimed. "I saw you laying here and I wasn't sure whether you were hurt or just sleeping so I gave you what I thought was a gentle poke."

"My apologies, I just got off the trail and felt this was a good place to camp for the night. I thought I would rest for a few minutes, but I must have fallen into a deep sleep."

"Oh, you were asleep alright. I didn't see you move a muscle, so I was concerned."

"What time is it?"

"Just after five."

"Holy Molly, I intended to have a five-minute power nap. I must have been out for over an hour."

"Hiking and fresh air will do that to us city dwellers."

After a few minutes of more chit chat Julech asked, "Would you care to join me for a bite to eat?"

"I'd love to, but I want to go further down the path before dark. I have to be back at the Lodge by mid-day tomorrow, so I need to get a couple of more hours in before I call it a day. Thanks for the offer. Now that I see you are alright, I'll be on my way. Happy trails to you."

"'Happy trails to you.' Who does he think he is, Roy Rogers?" Julech said under his breath.

"There's a nice clearing about three hours away. I stopped there for lunch. If you make it that far, you should be back in town by noon. Keep safe and thank you for your concern."

With that, Jake trudged down the path.

Now that he was fully awake and had his bearings once again, Julech looked at the pool of water. It was clear and inviting. He removed his clothes and dipped in his feet. The water was warm. He went all in and washed off the day's dust and sweat.

After his pool-bath, he cleared a spot for a fire, picked stones to make a circle for it, and gathered some dead branches and dry grass. Soon he had sufficient embers to put on a small pot of water.

He pulled out a package of dried vegetable soup, threw it into the pot and waited for it to boil. He mixed some flour, powdered milk, a teaspoon of baking powder, and pinch of salt. He spooned the ingredients into a frying pan and put it over the flame. With that he had made a couple of biscuits to complement his soup. In about 15 minutes his supper was ready. It wasn't a gourmet meal, but it was a hiker's meal. Out in the woods it tasted darn good.

While he was eating he noticed something move out of the corner of his eye. He had a visitor. A chipmunk was peeking over a rock with his nose twitching in the air. The smell of the biscuit is what got its attention. Julech broke off a piece of his biscuit and threw it about half way between him and the chipmunk.

"Come and get it," he whispered.

The chipmunk didn't look more than a year old. It was smaller than a squirrel, reddish in color, and had five dark stripes and several white stripes on its back. It looked like it could be a frisky fellow.

He decided to call him Chippy.

Chippy seemed fearless and crept up to the piece of biscuit, gobbled it down, and stared back at Julech as if to say, "Is that all there is?"

Julech broke off another piece and threw it closer to him. Chippy moved forward, grabbed the hunk of biscuit and in short order dashed up a tree. From there he kept a close eye on the guy below.

Julech could almost hear him say, "See you in the morning."

After he had finished his meal and washed the dishes, Julech leaned back against a stump. The evening was still, no bugs and the birds seemed to have called it a day. His mind went to his regular evening routine.

*   *   *

Julech had three habits he followed every day. They grew out of his experience while at The Abbey. Every morning he spent 30 to 45 minutes in spiritual reading and meditation, and every evening reviewed his day and planned for the next.

That morning's meditation took him to a place where he tried to understand the relationship between him and his God. Hence, he kept coming back to the questions, "Are you up there? Or, are you down there?"

As he reviewed those two questions again, he grew still and silent.

"Listen deeply," he remembered the bearded one saying.

He sat for a long time and then he thought he heard, "You are made in my image and my likeness."

He jumped up. Looked around. No one was there but him.

"That's from the first book of Genesis," he said to himself.

After a few more minutes of silence he cried out, "I'm made in the image of God."

He began to sort out the meaning of that message.

"I can't be God, but I can be made in his image. What does that mean?"

Julech had understood that an image is a visual representation of something. It reflected something that existed, like when someone looked into a mirror or saw himself in a photograph. The image wasn't the actual person who looked into the mirror or who was imprinted on the photograph, yet neither image would exist if the person didn't exist. The image received its meaning because it reflected something that already existed.

Julech's mind went into overdrive.

"If I'm made in the image of God, then somehow I must reflect that image. There must be something about me that is the same as God. Perhaps some form of indwelling of that image. Maybe that is what meant by the indwelling of the Spirit.

That's it! God is not up there, or down there. He is right here dwelling within me. And, if he is dwelling within me, He can never leave me.

God cannot come and go like I do. He can only exist as a being, as an ever present 'Ising'. And, since He can only Be, there can be no 'come and go.' Nor can He have a beginning and an end. If He had a beginning and an end He could not be an 'Ising'.

I am a distinct living person. I'm not like a photograph, I'm not static. So if I'm a representation of His image, it has to do with life. Maybe that's it, I share life. Or better, He shares His life with me because I'm made in His image. It is His life that allows me to breathe. His life must somehow reside within me. Not physically but spiritually. He is with me, in my spiritual core, for all time and eternity and in some way, I must have been with Him before my first breath. He is part of my spiritual DNA."

Julech sat back and let that sink in.

"I only have meaning and even life, because I reflect a Being which exists beyond me, whom I call God."

Julech knew that all major religions called upon a source beyond humanity's existence. They had different names for that source but there was something common about all of them.

Did he just get a hint of what might be 'common'?

He thought that if everyone was made in God's image, that must mean the core source of all human kind was the same. And if we were all made in the same image, then why was human-kind so divided? Why did we break into tribes, put others down, or place one nation over another? Why were we so divisive in our own communities?

These were questions to explore at another time. The question he thought he needed to discern first was what did 'likeness' mean and how did it relate to image.

Julech put his head in his hands. He had heard a voice that seemed to come from outside himself, but it was a voice that came from within him. He thought he understood with a bit more clarity where his God resided.

"Listen deeper."

*   *   *

Chippy poked his head out from under the leaves and gave a loud chip-chip yell. He wanted another piece of biscuit.

"No more for you until morning."

And with that Julech turned his attention to prepare for a night under the stars.

He placed the tarp on the ground, rolled out his sleeping bag, and put a pot of water on the dying embers to boil for a cup of tea.

He reviewed the day as he sipped his tea. The weather was perfect, he met an interesting bearded hiker, the day's hike took him to a beautiful spot where he had lunch, he found this place to settle down for the night, met Jake who was concerned about him, and ate with Chippy. He had a good day.

Before leaving on his journey, he calculated that with 15 kilos on his back he should be able to easily hike about 20 kilometres a day which translated into 3 kilometres an hour. He figured he hiked about 18 kilometres that day.

"Not bad for a first day. Tomorrow I will add another couple of kilometres."

He doused the fire with the remaining water in his canister and hit the sack.

He looked up to the vast sky with its bright stars flashing everywhere and said, "You are not up there. You are here within me, and I with You. Good night my God." With that, Julech felt he listened a little more deeply. He closed his eyes and fell asleep.

Not far away Chippy yawned and settled down for the night too.

So, ended the first day.

Maranatha

Julech opened one eye. A meter away, Chippy stared at him.

"Well, good morning to you too," laughed Julech.

It was light out, but the sun hadn't yet peeked over the mountain top. He checked his watch. It was close to six o'clock.

"T'is time to get up and start the day."

Chippy looked at him, bewildered. His day had already started.

Julech wandered over to the pool, splashed water on his face and brushed his teeth. He found more dead branches, picked some dried grass and lit a fire. He pulled out the couple biscuits he had made, dried egg powder, dried pieces of fruit, coffee grounds, powdered milk and an energy bar.

"That should do it for breakfast," he said to Chippy.

First, though as was his practice, he began to meditate. He usually began his meditation by closing his eyes, sitting straight on a chair, focusing on one word, and breathing gently. Sometimes that was easy to do, other times his mind jumped from one idea to another. The Buddha called this type of mind activity the "monkey mind".

Julech had learned that Buddha hadn't considered himself a holy man. He was someone who had great insight into human nature and the human mind. Experience had taught him that he could slow down his mind through meditation. He described the mind as filled with drunken monkeys all running around screeching, chattering, and begging for attention. He became convinced that everyone had monkey minds.

It was useless to fight the monkeys or try to bargain with them because somehow, they would always prevail. Instead, Buddha taught his followers to spend time each day in quiet meditation. He instructed them to simply calm the mind by focusing on breathing or repeating a simple mantra. In time, they could tame those monkeys by patiently and lovingly bringing them into submission.

Julech's drifted to thoughts about meditation in the Christian tradition.

In early c. 200 some Christians withdrew from society and sought their God in the desert. They became known as the Desert Fathers. They lived a simple and austere life. Many of them chose silence in a hermitage, while others formed communities. It was in the desert where the ancient practice of *lectio divina* (Latin for "divine reading") began.

For the Dessert Fathers *Lectio Divina* was an unhurried, contemplative reading of parts of Scripture. It gave them a basis to experience the Scriptural Word through meditation and contemplation.

Julech had read that there were four steps to *Lectio Divina*. First, the Desert Fathers read a Scripture passage slowly and kept an open and listening heart. As they read they looked for a word or phrase that struck them as if their God spoke to them directly. They concentrated on that phrase or word until they began the second step – a meditative process. During that step they chewed over the word or phrase and sought how it might apply to them. In the third step they prayed or simply and intimately conversed with their God. In the final step the Desert Fathers invoked a state of contemplation where they rested in silence and listened to what was spoken to them through their reading and meditation.

Three hundred years later around c.500, a person from Nursia, St Benedict (480 – 547) also left the noise of city life and founded the first Benedictine Monastery at Monte Cassino. St. Benedict wrote rules for communal living known as the Benedictine Rule. He became the father of monasticism and the Benedictine Rule became the norm for monastic living through-out Europe and gradually for the rest of the western world.

Fast forward to the Monks of The Abbey. Every morning they diligently meditated. After chanting morning *Lauds*, they would settle back in their pews, calm their minds and enter into a quiet contemplative state.

The Monks of The Abbey were the first to teach Julech about meditation. They followed the steps of *Lectio Divina*, but when he attempted that method his monkeys became disturbed. He thought about all the possibilities the readings suggested, but then got so engrossed in the story that he continued to read rather than meditate.

Years later, while on a business trip to England he attended a lecture at the University of London featuring another Benedictine monk. He reminded his audience about the impor-tance of quieting the monkeys with a mantra. He referenced an ancient Christian greeting, *Maranatha,* meaning the Lord Comes. He instructed to say it with four syllables *Ma/ra/na/tha.*

"Breath normally and give your full attention to the word as you say it, silently, gently, faithfully and simply," he said.

Julech made the mantra his own and translated it to mean, "Come Lord, I'm listening." Obviously, though, according to the bearded hiker, Julech still had much to learn about listening deeper.

Julech had observed that meditation was simple in nature yet transcended thought when one controlled the monkeys. When people were in that state, they existed in the moment, and in that moment, time was suspended. They went beyond consciousness and were gifted with the whisper of the divine where compassion, respectfulness and forgiveness were strengthened.

Julech rolled all those meditative methods around in his head and realized that the monkeys were busy. He had wandered off on the history and methods of meditation and hadn't entered into a quiet meditative state.

"Focus," he said to himself.

He sat up straight, fixed his sight on a bright yellow buttercup glistening with morning dew drops and repeated the word *Maranatha*.

*   *   *

About 30 minutes later he heard a sharp chip-chip noise. It was Chippy up in the tree sending a strong message in chipmunkese,

"Where's my biscuit you promised me last night?"

Julech looked at the supplies he had laid out, stoked the fire and placed water to boil for coffee. He had a habit of drinking coffee in the morning. Strong black coffee boiled on an open camp fire was the best.

He mixed powdered milk and eggs in the frying pan to make scrambled eggs and placed the biscuits on top of the eggs to heat them.

Chippy crept closer. He wanted a piece of that biscuit.

Julech had something better to give him. He pulled out a few nuts from his backpack and held them out.

"If you want these, you will have to come and get them," coaxed Julech.

Slowly Chippy crawled up to his hand, filled his cheeks with the nuts and then ran like a 'bat out of hell' up a tree.

It wasn't long before Chippy was back. He looked at Julech with his big eyes. Again, Julech extended his hand with nuts. This time Chippy wasn't so slow. He jumped on Julech's knee and put his paws into Julech's hands and took the nuts.

After breakfast, Julech poured water over the coals, packed the utensils, frying pan and a left-over biscuit into his backpack. He refilled his water canister, tightened up his boots, and put on his *Chapeau*. He was ready for another day of hiking.

He looked around to say goodbye to Chippy, but Chippy was nowhere in sight.

"Oh well, he's probably off telling his friends about the feast he had for breakfast."

Julech shouted out a goodbye anyway and headed up the trail.

"It's going to be another beautiful day. No clouds, no wind and thankfully, no bugs."

He felt a tinge of soreness in his legs and muscles from yesterday's hike, so he planned to hike in one-and-half-hour spurts rather than in three-hour marathons. He wanted to take the first hour slowly and then gradually speed up his gait. He figured the time he lost in the first hour could be made up in the afternoon.

When Julech began his hike, he was heading southward toward the sun. The valley was on the east side of him and he was able to see it for most of that day. Somewhere before he stopped for camp the trail shifted toward the west and the valley receded. Now he was hiking directly west, and he had to turn around to see the valley. It was still in sight but off in the distance. The next time he looked back he could only see the trees on the side of the opposite mountain. The valley had disappeared.

He was now fully on the deer path of long ago. There was little sound except for the birds on each side of him.

"I wonder how many deer traveled this path and how many hunters followed them?" he quizzed. The question reminded him of Sam Walter Foss's (1858-1911) poem, *The Calf-Path*.

I

One day through the primeval wood
A calf walked home as good calves should;

But made a trail all bent askew,
A crooked trail as all calves do.

Since then three hundred years have fled,
And I infer the calf is dead.

II.

But still he left behind his trail,
And thereby hangs my moral tale.

The trail was taken up next day,
By a lone dog that passed that way;

And then a wise bell-wether sheep
Pursued the trail o'er vale and steep,

And drew the flock behind him, too,
As good bell-wethers always do.

And from that day, o'er hill and glade,
Through those old woods a path was made.

III.

And many men wound in and out,
And dodged, and turned, and bent about,

And uttered words of righteous wrath,
Because 'twas such a crooked path;

But still they followed – do not laugh –
The first migrations of that calf.

And through this winding wood-way stalked
Because he wobbled when he walked.

IV.

This forest path became a lane,
That bent and turned and turned again;

This crooked lane became a road,
Where many poor horse with his load

Toiled on beneath the burning sun,
And traveled some three miles in one.

And thus a century and a half
They trod the footsteps of that calf.

V.

The years passed on in swiftness fleet,
The road became a village street;

And this, before men were aware,

A city's crowded thoroughfare.

And soon the central street was this
Of a renowned metropolis;

And men two centuries and a half,
Trod the footsteps of that calf.

VI.

Each day a hundred thousand rout
Followed the zigzag calf about

And o'er his crooked journey went
The traffic of a continent.

A Hundred thousand men were led,
By one calf near three centuries dead.

They followed still his crooked way,
And lost one hundred years a day;

For thus such reverence is lent,
To well established precedent.

VII

A moral lesson this might teach
Were I ordained and called to preach;

For men are prone to go it blind
Along the calf-paths of the mind,

And work away from sun to sun,

To do what other men have done.

They follow in the beaten track,
And out and in, and forth and back,

And still their devious course pursue,
To keep the path that others do.

They keep the path a sacred groove,
Along which all their lives they move.

But how the wise old wood gods laugh,
Who saw the first primeval calf.

Ah, many things this tale might teach –
But I am not ordained to preach.

Julech smiled to himself as he reflected on the poem and on his morning meditation.

"From monkeys screaming and bouncing around in my mind to deeply furrowed calf paths. One reminiscent of a mind that was overly active and disquieting, while the other was ponderous and unchanging," he said to himself.

*   *   *

Crack!
Julech jumped. He turned and searched the trees. He cautiously moved forward and kept his eyes southward toward those trees.

Another crack, quieter this time. He kept walking. More rustling and cracking, then nothing. Silence.

He gingerly took more steps.

Stopped.

Listened.

Nothing.

Silence.

He moved at a faster pace and looked sideways. He couldn't see anything, nor could he hear any noise. Perhaps – a deer, a calf or a monkey?

"Enough of that," he said to himself and pushed on.

When he broke camp earlier it was cool, so he kept his pant legs zipped at the knees. It had warmed considerably since then. He looked at his watch. He had been hiking for about two hours. A half hour longer than he had planned. The kinks in his leg muscles had loosened and stretched themselves out.

He saw a large stump ahead. A good place to stop and rest.

Julech pulled the energy bar and a piece of dried fruit from his pocket. He looked around. All was still. He zipped off his pant legs and proceeded to shove them into his pack.

A loud screeching noise came from within, and out jumped Chippy.

Julech couldn't understand chipmunk swearing but if he could he was sure Chippy was yelling, "!@$#* it was hot in there! You could've let me out sooner. It seems to me that was pretty damn inconsiderate of you."

"Hey, take it easy! I didn't know you were in there. I thought you left me to tell your friends about the great breakfast you had."

"Great breakfast, ha! You were stingy on the nuts and you didn't even give me a piece of your biscuit."

"What the heck is this for gawd sake, I'm arguing with a chipmunk," Julech said as he rolled his eyes.

After breakfast that morning, while Julech was in the bush taking care of business, Chippy had hopped into the backpack hoping to pilfer some more nuts. Before he was able to get out,

Julech came back, closed the cover of the pack, flung it on his back and started off.

Chippy couldn't do anything but go along for the ride and catch a little shut eye. But boy was it hot in there and he couldn't even find where Julech kept the nuts.

Julech opened his backpack and found the container of nuts. He noticed that Chippy made a neat little nest in the corner where he had curled up to sleep. He gently removed the container without disturbing the nest. He sensed that Chippy was going to ride with him for the rest of the journey.

While Julech rummaged around in the pack, Chippy scampered into the trees. This time Chippy had to take care of some business. Soon he was back sitting next to Julech.

Julech stretched out his hand with a couple of nuts. Chippy jumped onto his knee and packed them into his mouth. He then poured water into the lid of the nut container and held it for the chipmunk.

Chippy drank until there wasn't a drop left. He finally cooled down and looked quizzically at Julech.

"Now what?" Julech asked.

In true chipmunk language, Chippy said, "I'm not going back in there, but I'm going with you, Julech."

Julech remembered Catrela telling him about a friend of hers who had a baby skunk. That skunk went everywhere with her friend. Stinky, the Skunk's name, would sit on her shoulders, on top of her head, or in her pocket. It scared the living day lights out of people when it poked its head out.

"I think Chippy is going to be like Stinky," Julech said to himself.

Chippy stood on the stump.

Julech slung on his backpack, put an almond on his shoulder and extended his hand and arm out to him.

Chippy took the hint and scampered up his arm, grabbed the almond and jumped onto the top of his Hat. He surveyed the land and said to himself in chipmunkese, "This is a fine perch, I'm going to sit and watch from here."

"Boy for a rodent you sure catch on fast."

Chippy smiled as chipmunks do and chipped, "I'm smarter than you think. By the way I'll do anything for an almond."

Julech pulled out his phone and took a Selfie and then headed up the trail.

The path twisted and turned and in places increased its slope and then dipped downward and back upward again. It felt like the calf-path.

*   *   *

Julech's mind drifted back to the methods of mediations he had worked through earlier. Another one popped into his head. It was called *Japa*. Those who practiced the *Japa* method were encouraged to seek silence, concentrate on the space between two words and recite a mantra.

Julech remembered his Japa teacher telling him,

> "Picture a sentence or phrase such as 'love your neighbor as yourself.' Repeat the phrase, 'love your neighbor as yourself,' and while repeating it, drop off the end word 'yourself.' Slowly repeat the phrase and gradually drop off a word until you arrive at the two words 'love your.' Then separate the two words and move into the space between the words. Let the words 'love' and 'your' become the bookends for the space. During the process of getting into the space, repeat a simple mantra for example, *Love* or *Maranatha* either softly out loud or within your mind."

Julech had practiced the three methods of Buddha Mindfulness, *Japa*, and *Lectio Divina* and in time he found they supported and complemented one another. That was his 'aha' meditation moment.

He employed the different techniques throughout his life. Some days he would read then mediate (*Lectio Divina)*; other days he would use the *Japa* technique. He found the *Japa* technique particularly helpful when he wanted to take a three to five-minute break. He would take one minute to form a phrase, one minute to move out of his monkey world and into the space between the two words, one minute to concentrate on his mantra and one minute to recover. They became refreshing five-minute breaks at work, or when he was waiting for someone.

"You know Chippy, there were times when Catrela was talking to me and I was in *Japa* mode. It seemed to her that I wasn't in the room, I was somewhere else. The stern, 'I'm talking to you,' or 'Are you listening to me?' usually brought me back to earth."

Chippy opened one eye and mumbled, "Good for her."

The sun had reached mid-day. It was noon and time to stop for lunch.

Chippy had moved from the Hat to his shoulder and curled up between the pack and his back. He slept most of the way since they had their mid-morning break, except when Julech referred to him about his meditation techniques.

When Julech bent down to lift off his backpack, Chippy woke up, chip-chipped, yawned and leapt off his shoulder. All he wanted was nuts.

Julech hadn't planned on feeding rodents with nuts. He only packed enough to supplement his diet. At the rate Chippy was eating them, they would last about two more days.

As he stuck his hand into the pack to get his lunch, he muttered, "No more nuts for you Chippy. You are now rationed to three nuts a day."

Chippy looked at him. He didn't understand what he said and chip-chipped again. He didn't get any nuts. Instead, Julech handed him a piece of his biscuit. He looked at Julech and in chipmunkese demanded nuts.

"Eat the biscuit! And be grateful for that."

He could almost hear a sigh of resignation as Chippy took the biscuit.

After the noon break the two were off again.

Julech's legs had fully recovered. They allowed him to march with strength and determination. As he put one foot in front of the other he savored the sounds, smells and sights that surrounded him.

The afternoon heat and the weight of the pack was getting to Julech. It was time he looked for a place to camp for the night.

Just as those thoughts crossed his mind, he saw an opening on a ridge with a flowing stream and a cascading waterfall.

Julech stopped and pitched camp.

The timing had been perfect and so was the site. The mist from the fall provided a soothing relief as it brushed over Julech's sweaty body. Chippy enjoyed it too as he pushed his head into the mist. They both rested on the ground with a contented grin on their faces.

"I'll bet there are some fish at the bottom of those falls," he said to Chippy.

"Fish? What would I do with fish?"

Julech pulled out some tackle and fishhooks from his pack. Sauntered over to the bush and chopped off a straight branch.

"That should reach about the middle of the creek," he said to himself. "Now to find an insect."

It didn't take him long to trap a grasshopper between his hands, put it on a hook and cast the line below the falls. An hour later he had caught two 10-inch rainbow trout and couldn't wait until he pan fried them.

While Julech fished, Chippy explored. He dashed around until almost dizzy. He hadn't stretched his legs for a long time. He ran up and down trees, scampered beneath the underbrush, climbed rocks and scratched for mealworms.

"Mealworms are better than fish."

After he had his fill, he followed his nose back to camp. Something was cooking.

Chippy watched with interest as Julech fried his fish, boiled some powdered potatoes and dried beans. He was even more interested when Julech began to eat his meal.

"How could he eat that," he chipped. "Mealworms were much better!"

He ran off to dig for some more.

"There's nothing like fresh pan-fried rainbow trout. Now for a good cup of coffee and a bit of fruit," Julech said in his best outdoorsman voice.

Chippy smelled the coffee brewing. He had learned that when Julech drank coffee there was always something accompanying it. He followed his nose back to camp.

He saw Julech chomping on some dried fruit. Now dried fruit was something that Chippy could stomach.

He jumped on Julech's knee and held out his paws. Julech picked out a piece of dried apricot and gave it to him. Apricots happened to be Chippy's favorite fruit. He gulped a chunk down in three bites.

The rodent and the man filled with awe and pleased about the day sat and watched the sun set. Julech found a marvelous traveling companion, and Chippy found a trusting big person who was willing to share his pack of goodies. They spoke different languages, but they seemed to understand each other completely.

Julech reviewed his musings about meditation and the benefits he derived from it.

"You know Chippy, since spending quiet time in meditation I have experienced less stress and I believe have become more open to others."

"Good for you," Chippy said in a way that meant "You don't have to tell me about it."

It occurred to Julech that he would be meditating more than usual on this journey.

The sun dropped behind the mountain, the air got cooler and the fire burned down to a soft white ash. Julech and Chippy settled in for the night. Julech in his sleeping bag, and Chippy in the corner of the pack.

And so, ended the second day.

Love's Diamond

It was day break and light ended the dark night. The two new found friends woke up to the early morning songs of meadowlarks, robins, wrens, starlings, sparrows and a few ravens cackling in the background trying to drown out the rest of the choir.

Chippy thrust his head out of the pack, looked around and said, "You can get up. It's too early for me. Go do your meditation, I'm alright with God." With that he disappeared back to his cozy corner.

Julech stretched and muttered, "What a way to start the morning."

Sometimes Julech would randomly open a Scripture passage to kick start his meditation. He flipped to the New Testament on his smartphone and read a passage from Matthew:

"Therefore I tell you, do not worry about your life, what you will eat or drink; or about your body, what you will wear. Is not life more than food, and the body more than clothes? Look at the birds of the air; they do not sow or reap or store away in barns, and yet your heavenly Father feeds them. Are you not much more valuable than they? Can any one of you by worrying add a single hour to your life?" (Matthew 6: 25-27)

Chippy didn't worry nor did the morning song birds. Chippy was right, he *was alright with God.*

Julech chewed over those two verses and wondered how they might apply to him. He settled on the word 'worry'.

Why do I worry? Worry doesn't get me anywhere. All it seems to do is make me anxious, nervous and edgy and sometimes even neurotic and fearful. Maybe that's it, it's about fear. Fear of what? Fear of losing my money, friends, mind, life, control, power; or, becoming ill, old, or homeless; or making a mistake, or obsessing about what people might say or think of me. There is no end of things I can fear or worry about.

"Fear is the elephant's mouse," Catrela often said.

As Julech considered the meaning behind the passage he resolved that it wasn't worth worrying about the things he didn't control or tying himself up in knots with unfounded fear. That didn't get him anywhere.

He looked at the passage again and another notion emerged, that of faith in the 'Father.' It seemed to him that Jesus may have been implying that faith in his 'Father' would overcome worry and fear. It was like, "Don't worry my Father will take care of it or have faith my Father will take care of everything."

The passage seemed to link fear with faith. It struck him that both fear and faith dealt with the future.

He had observed that when people viewed the future with fear they experienced less energy and became pessimistic, negative and distrustful. However, when they viewed the future with faith they became more up-beat, hopeful, optimistic and trustful.

He asked himself, "Was Jesus saying have a deep faith in his Father and things will work out?" and then quickly answered.

"I don't think this is about not doing anything and expect the 'Father" to do everything for me. I have to do something about my worry or fear. I have to uncover the root causes of my worries and fears and remove them. That I can do with confidence and faith in the Father."

He began softly chanting *Maranatha*.

*　　*　　*

After Chippy had hit the snooze button for another thirty minutes more sleep, he woke up and loudly shouted his chip-chip "breakfast time!"

That yell broke Julech from his trance.

"Boy, I sure don't need a bell to ring to end my meditation with you around."

Julech lit a fire, put on a pot to boil water for coffee and oatmeal. Chippy liked oatmeal, however he preferred it dry rather than cooked.

They sat in silence, ate their breakfast and listened to nature's wake up calls.

Julech got up and went off to the bush to take care of business.

He had just settled when he heard a piercing screeching noise. It was in chipmunkese.

"My gawd, something's happened to Chippy!"

He rushed to put his pants on but wasn't too successful. He hopped and skipped back to the site with one pant leg on and the other dragging behind him.

There was Chippy in fine form. He was swearing over Julech's cup of coffee. He wanted a drink, but the coffee was, in Chippy's language "too #@%&* hot!"

Julech laughed at the scene, picked up his cup, poured coffee in a bowl, added water to cool it, and gave it to him. Chippy's hot temper soon cooled down as well.

Julech rolled up the sleeping bag, doused the fire, gathered the utensils, put them in his pack and lifted the pack onto his back.

Chippy jumped onto Julech's shoulder, picked up a peanut and hopped to the top of the *Chapeau*. A spot which now had become his navigational perch.

They were off for another day of hiking

The two continued to travel in a westerly direction. The temperature was perfect for climbing up an inclining pathway. Julech hoped that their early start would result in making up a few of the kilometres he lost over the last couple of days. He planned to continue to hike in 90-minute spurts and after 15 or 20 minutes rest they would push on.

The fresh smell of the evergreens and the leggy grass heavy with the morning dew pleasantly tickled Julech's nostrils. Chippy even twitched his nose as he stood tall on the Hat.

Chippy was used to the forest aromas. He often woke up to this type of morning during the summer. Julech didn't, so he breathed in the pungent scents and savored the moment.

Maybe, Julech thought with a smile, the bearded man should have added "smell deeper" to his counsel.

*   *   *

With an openness to faith Julech turned his mind back to the first evening of the journey when he reflected on the "image and likeness" of God. His insight about the image of God had made sense to him, but what about "likeness"? What did that mean?

"After all, when I see my image in a mirror isn't it a likeness of me?"

His meditation had led him to believe that he was made in the image of God and at his core he was one with God, or more correctly, God was one with him as Spirit.

"God is at the core of who I am. But what did He mean when He said I'm made in His 'likeness'?"

He knew likeness was comparable to an image, but could likeness mean something different?

As he labored up the trail he saw two flowers that were alike. They appeared to be checkerblooms. They had five petals and many stamens. Their leaves were shaped in the form of a maple leaf at the bottom and were broader at the top. Although they came from the same botanical family they were different. One flower was blue and the other a lily white These were the attributes of the flower. Each an image of the other, but not of the same likeness or attributes.

> "Aha!" shouted Julech. "That must be it. God's Image and likeness are bound within the same Being. His image relates more to His substance and His likeness relates more to His attributes. Since I am made in the 'image and likeness' of God I must also have those same attributes dwelling within me. Does this mean at my core I possess the attributes of justice, love, joy, forgiveness, mercy and goodness? And if I do, then the real question for me is do 'I reflect those attributes outward to others?' or to put it another way, 'do I imitate those attributes in my relationships with others?"

Julech likened all God's attributes to the facets of a diamond. Each facet poured out the inner beauty of the diamond and each one reflected the brilliance of the whole and couldn't be separated from it else it diminished the sparkling shine of the whole diamond.

> "Could it be, because I am made in the image of God, my job is to become 'like' God by practicing those facets of the diamond? Is this what Jesus meant when he talked about loving both your neighbor and your enemies and going beyond just loving those we know (Matthew 5:43-47). Was he asking us to do more?"

Julech thought of all the attributes attributed to God he would concentrate on God as Love.

In Julech's mind love was the fire that incubated and vibrated the diamond's radiance. It was the fire of the Spirit that pulsated Love which allowed him to say, 'God is Love'. And if God is Love, He could only radiate love. He could "not love" and therefore must love everybody and everything, even those who harmed another or who claimed that He didn't exist.

Julech tucked those thoughts away and would come back to them later. He had come to the end of his first 90-minute trek and stopped to rest beside a trickling creek.

*   *   *

He stooped down to take a drink from the creek and Chippy jumped off his perch to join him.

Julech sat down on the grass and lifted his legs up on a rock to give them rest.

Chippy, who had hardly moved his legs for the past hour and half, ran under the bushes, up and down a pine tree and jumped over stumps and logs. He then saddled up to Julech for a piece of the energy bar that he was eating.

Thirty minutes later they were back on the trail.

The sun beat down on Julech and Chippy. The towering trees on each side of the path soothed them with shade. It was a much cooler climb than yesterday.

They hiked for another two 90-minute stretches and landed at a clearing that looked like a place where deer or cattle had grazed. Flowers dotted the ground everywhere and busy honey bees flitted from one flower to another.

Julech and Chippy settled down for lunch and a welcomed break. Off in the distance he heard a haunting, trilling sound and guessed it might be a thrush trying to entice a mate. He looked around and there it was sitting on a branch.

A black band crossed its rusty-orange breast. It had a black head and a bright orange stripe behind its eye. Its sides appeared salty looking and there were splashes of orange in its wings. These marking confirmed to Julech that it was indeed a thrush of the varied kind.

The buzzing of the bees caught Julech's attention. He knew bees had an impressive system. Most of them were worker bees that toiled as a team. The bee team worked inside a beehive and the outer layer of the hive formed the boundaries within which the team operated. In the wild, bees used caves, rock cavities and hollow trees to form their nests. The nests were usually composed of several honeycombs with a single entrance. Inside the nests the bees worked together and produced their product – beeswax and honey.

All the bees within the nest had a clear role to play which changed as they aged. They started out as housekeepers, and grew into undertakers, baby sitters, worker bees and field bees. And, of course, there was the queen bee.

Julech watched the field bees as they bounced from one flower to the next, pollinating them as they went and then flying off with their heavy loads back to the nest.

He looked at Chippy.

"Let's go find the nest and sneak some honey for our cereal."

"Are you sure? Bee stings aren't pleasant."

"You're right. Bee stings aren't pleasant."

Watching the bees reminded Julech of the bumble bees that visited Catrela every summer. She would talk to them and especially the little ones as they buzzed from one flower pot to another. Julech remembered her telling him that she was concerned about the bees. She had noticed that as each year passed there were fewer bees than the previous year.

"She would be pleased at the sight of these bees," he said to Chippy.

"What are you talking about?"

The morning coolness had long gone, and now the afternoon sun was hot. It got hotter as Julech trudged along the path. Ever since he left the small meadow where they had lunch he noticed that he was hiking in a steep upward direction. The trees had receded from the path which allowed more open space for the sun to shine through. The heat from the sun had begun to take its toll on Julech.

To get away from the heat, Chippy, moved off the Hat and jumped down to the ground. He followed Julech along the grass and underbrush that lined the path. About every half-hour the two would stop and replenish themselves with water, and Julech would pour some over his and Chippy's head. That was something new for Chippy and Julech could tell he enjoyed the splashes of coolness.

*   *   *

All afternoon, Julech came back to the theme of 'God's image and likeness'. He had appreciated in broad terms how he could participate in the attributes of justice, love, joy, forgiveness, mercy and goodness.

However the other attributes associated with God such as all knowing, powerful, present, infinite, eternal and unchanging still posed questions for him.

Some people he knew gave the impression they 'knew it all,' and sought after 'might and power'; and the way they acted and hoarded their riches he wondered if they thought they would never die.

His mind began to churn.

> "We can search for knowledge and learn to live in the present, but we could never attain the 'fullness of knowledge' nor the 'fullness of presence', as we understand God to have or else we would be God.
>
> I'll leave the qualities of an all-powerful, infinite, eternal and unchanging God for another time. I know all these attributes must come together at some point. For now the question is: how do they bring meaning and purpose to my life?
>
> The one path I see that makes most sense to me is to contribute to the wellbeing of others by pursuing the qualities of love, forgiveness, mercy, and goodness. However, there is a proviso and that is precisely because I'm human, I don't think I can measure up to the fullness of those qualities."

He harkened back to his morning's meditation and realized that this proviso wasn't something he should worry about. "What I can do is to strive to become the best person I can be by applying them to the best of my ability," he concluded.

*   *   *

Julech and Chippy must have hiked for at least 25 kilometres. His legs had become weak, and his shoulders sore. Both legs and shoulders felt the weight of hauling the backpack. It was time to stop for the day.

He saw a small opening nestled up against a rocky cliff. The trail took them in a north westerly direction, but the clearing allowed them to look directly west over the trees.

Julech plopped his pack down and as he did Chippy jumped from his shoulder to a near-by stump. He shook his legs and hopped about. It looked as if he was getting his land legs back after the afternoon of navigating on top his perch. He also wasn't that tired as he had slept in the crook between the pack and the back of Julech's neck. He was frisky and ready to run around. Julech on the other hand was dead tired. He flopped down, put his head on his pack and in no time was fast asleep.

Chippy investigated this new place. He scurried up the rocky cliff and surveyed the forest below. There wasn't much that interested him down there, so he scrounged around the rocks for something to eat. Outside of a few insects, which he didn't like, he found a few mushrooms. He tasted them and quickly spit them out. He didn't like those either. He went back down the cliff and followed his nose to the edge of the alcove. He crept further under the brush. There they were: wild strawberries and a whole patch of them.

"Now that's something I can eat!" He laid back and picked them off one by one.

Meanwhile, Julech was fast asleep and hadn't heard the porcupine lumbering up behind his head. It scratched on the pack. Julech stirred. The porcupine clicked his teeth, pushed out its quills and swatted its tail on the ground. That got Julech's attention.

Julech had heard that noise before when he hiked overnight with his young scouts near the Kokanee Glaciers. Porcupines were nocturnal rodents and around mid-night they had invaded their camp. The teenagers were up most of the night chasing them away by clacking sticks together.

He was surprised to hear a porcupine so early in the evening.

Julech slowly moved his hand out and grabbed a rock. He tried to lay still. The porcupine didn't budge. Its clicking noises and tail pounding became louder.

"This is not good," thought Julech.

He kept quiet. Maybe the critter, which now grew to become a 'beast' in his mind, would leave. It seemed like an hour, but probably only about ten minutes when the porcupine moseyed off.

Julech sat up but kept the rock in his hand. The porcupine was about 10 Kilograms in weight. It looked back, turned, straightened its quills and aimed them at Julech. Julech threw the rock and hoped that would scare it away. It didn't. It came closer.

Julech knew porcupines had poor eye sight. He guessed it wanted a closer look.

Julech stepped back, picked up another rock and threw it. This time the rock had hit him in the head. The porcupine rolled over.

Julech only wanted to scare the 'beast' but the rock killed it. He was surprised at this turn of events. Porcupines were slow rodents and they were not supposed to be easy to kill. Certainly not by hitting one with a rock at the speed with which Julech threw it.

"Now what do I do with a dead porcupine?" he asked himself.

Julech had learned that porcupine meat was often used as survival food. A porcupine diet consisted of leaves, plants, twigs, and tree bark which meant that its meat was safe to eat. One could even eat the meat raw, but that certainly didn't appeal to Julech's appetite.

"We're going to have porcupine stew for supper! But how am I going to get it ready for the pot?"

Normally one carefully skinned a porcupine with heavy gloves and removed its spines with pliers. Julech had neither. He had to improvise.

He stuffed his hands into a pair of socks then wrapped them around the bottom half of his zipped off pant legs, and proceeded to operate on the prickly rodent. Patiently he removed the spines with the best pliers he had – those at the end of his Swiss Army Knife.

He skinned the fat off the carcass, chopped up a portion of the meat, and braised it in the frying pan. He poured water into a pot, threw in dried vegetables, powdered beef broth and the meat. He placed the pot onto the fire to boil. He estimated that it would take a couple of hours before the stew would be ready to eat.

Julech sliced the rest of the meat into bacon-like strips and fried them with the porcupine fat. Once they were cooked, he set them aside to dry and cool. After a while, he sprinkled them with salt and put them into a Ziplock bag. He had just made crisp slices of protein for the next few days.

He sat back and grinned. He looked at the boiling pot and the zip bag filled with porcupine meat. He was pleased with his butchering and culinary accomplishment.

As he sat looking at his boiling stew he realized that he had been so taken up with the porcupine episode that he forgot all about Chippy.

Chippy wasn't around.

He called for him but there was no chip-chip in return. He looked up into the trees and couldn't see anything but an old crow. He called again. No answer.

Julech wasn't too concerned about the whereabouts of Chippy. They had formed a close bond over the past couple of days and he felt he would return when his nose smelled the food cooking.

Julech's pant bottoms and socks were a mess from the porcupine operation. They needed to be washed. He gathered them in his arms and picked up a bar of soap. He wandered to the edge of the alcove where he had heard water flowing. There, he washed his clothes, while keeping an eye on the camp fire not too far away.

After washing his pants and socks and while he was getting up off his knees, he noticed a patch of red berries to his right. He not only saw ripe red wild strawberries, but also Chippy, sleeping on his belly with what looked like red lips and a smile on his face.

"Chippy! It's time to wake up. Supper will soon be on the table. And, what a supper it's going to be."

Chippy perked up his nose and smelled something strange.

"What in the world is that?"

On the way back to the boiling stew, Julech stopped to dig up a hand full of tender dandelions.

Back at the camp fire he poured water into a small pot and added a few tablespoons of powdered potatoes.

He turned to Chippy and said, "We're having porcupine stew with vegetables, potatoes and dandelion salad, topped off with strawberries for dessert. What more could a hiker in the wild wish to eat."

"Nuts," came the quick reply.

Chippy didn't like the stew meat, but he gobbled up a tiny portion of the vegetables, dandelions and strawberries. Julech enjoyed the whole meal and found the porcupine tasted like duck meat. It was tender and sweet. The strawberries were an added delicious treat.

They watched the sun, dressed in a bright golden tinge, fall behind the opposite mountain and prepared themselves for another night under the stars.

Chippy crawled into the pack and Julech slid into his bag.

Julech reviewed his day starting with the chorus of birds, his morning meditation about worry and fear being replaced with trust, optimism and hope, the insights about the attributes of God, the colorful thrush and busy bees, the episode with the porcupine, the tasty supper, and the magnificent sunset. A deep sense of amazement and appreciation came over him. He uttered a prayer of thanksgiving, not only for what he experienced that day, but also for Catrela who had graciously wished him well as he set out on his journey.

And so, ended the third day.

The Wonder of Love

IT WAS DAY BREAK, CLOUDY WITH A NORTH WESTERN WIND, AND cool. The temperature had dropped a few degrees and Julech felt like Chippy yesterday morning. He was warm wrapped up in his bag and wanted ten more minutes of shut eye. He closed his eyes and drifted back to sleep.

Chippy had already bounced out of the corner of the pack. He went for a morning run and ended up at the strawberry patch.

"Nothing like an early breakfast," he chipped.

After his fill of berries, he scampered back to camp, jumped on Julech's head and rustled his hair all the while chip chipping away.

Julech stretched.

"Alright, alright, I'll get up."

He crawled out of the sack, splashed water on his face and shook out the night cobwebs from his mind.

"It's about time." And with what looked like a silly grin, Chippy jumped back into the pack. He knew it was meditation time, so he just settled back in his corner, kept quiet and fell asleep and dreamt about strawberries.

*   *   *

Julech homed in on where he left off yesterday afternoon – God's love.

Love, for Julech, was an all-encompassing embrace that transcended everything. He believed in a Judeo-Christian God, who constantly poured out love to all of creation, giving it life and meaning. He reasoned that whenever he loved someone he participated in that great outpouring. He surmised that If God was at the center and the cause of all love, he couldn't live without God's love, and the love he had for others was but a likeness of God's love for him.

Julech continued to unravel his thoughts.

> "God can 'not love' but I can choose not to love God. I can also choose not to love myself or others. However, even if I did choose not to love God, myself or others, God still loves me. He is present with continual love keeping me "in the palms of his hands." (Is 49:36).

> God loves all regardless of human failings and wickedness, so if I rest in his love, I can learn to love those I dislike or those who harm me. Maybe that's why I have heard about people who can find love in the most hideous of places and in the ugliest of relationships. Yes, if I look I can even find reflections of love in prisons, ghettos, refugee camps and in the cruelty and ugliness of war and famine.

God's love knows no bounds, but boy is that hard
for me to fully comprehend."

Julech closed his meditation wondering how he could
contribute to resolving the injustices of the world caused by
poverty, racism and discrimination. He thought that if in some
small way he could help others see that we are all made in the
image of God, and at our core we are one with each other then
there would be no room for racism or discrimination. And, if
he truly clothed himself with love, then perhaps he too could
help alleviate some of the ills caused by poverty, bitterness,
hatred and conflict.

He thought of Mother Teresa, Francis of Assisi, Martin Luther
King, Mahatma Gandhi and all those who gave a hand up to the
less fortunate within their communities. He felt those giants
of the past and those living today drew strength and energy
from this Great Love.

"Maranatha," he chanted.

*   *   *

Chippy's dream of strawberries popped, and he woke up
twitching his nose. There was something burning. He poked his
head out of the pack and there was Julech frying "porcubacon"
– he didn't have pork bacon, but he did have porcupine strips
that looked like bacon. Chippy's nose didn't like the aroma. Oats,
nuts and berries had a much better smell. Although the smell
was a bit pungent, Julech didn't mind it. He looked forward to
a breakfast of scrambled eggs, porcubacon, and black coffee.

The wind had died down, but the sky was still puffy with
light clouds.

"We should make good time, today," he said to Chippy.

"Will we?".

Chippy wasn't certain where Julech was taking him on this journey, but he was enjoying the ride and Julech's company.

The path followed along the rocky ridge that started where they had camped. There was a steep stony wall on one side and a gully filled with evergreens, brush and tall grass on the other. The path was clear of debris and Julech guessed that it must have had a herd of deer tramping on it in recent days.

Chippy looked up into the sky and saw a hawk making wide circles looking for critters about his size. He got off the Hat and slouched beside Julech's neck. He kept one eye to the sky. The hawk was still there. He snuck between the pack and Julech's shoulder. He looked up. The hawk continued to hover over head.

Chippy began to chip-chip quietly.

Julech didn't pay much attention to the chip-chip, he was concentrating on the trail.

Chippy squeezed in between the flap and the pack and slid down to his corner and stayed there. He wasn't going to come out until Julech stopped for his morning break.

Julech slid his hand into his backpack to get his canister of water and felt his furry friend.

"What are you doing in there?"

Chippy didn't stir. Julech then heard the squawks of the hawk. He looked up. There on the top of a pine tree was a northern goshawk, with his alternating black and white puffy feathers and beady red eyes looking straight at Julech.

"Ah, now I understand."

Northern goshawks preyed on squirrels, rabbits, grouse and medium sized birds. Chippy came from the same squirrel family, so it wasn't rocket science to suggest that the goshawk might swoop down and gather him up.

"You're one smart critter to hide," Julech whispered.

"I know," came a muffled reply.

Julech wanted to get as far away from the goshawk as he could. He knew it had keen eyesight and would spot Chippy if he came out of the backpack. He kept walking and periodically looked to the tree tops and the sky. He wanted to ensure the bird was gone before he stopped for a rest.

The hawk had sensed there was a prey close by and continued to fly in circles above the hiker. The hiker hiked on until his legs could no longer carry him. He sat down beside the path and surveyed the sky and trees again. He couldn't see the hawk. It must have found another small animal or bird to appease his appetite.

Chippy crawled out of the pack, gasped, and chipped for water.

They sat on the cool ledge and Julech shared his nut coated energy bar with Chippy. Chippy was still nervous and kept his nose and eyes pointed upward. He relaxed when they were ready to go. There wasn't a goshawk in sight. He jumped to the top of the *Chapeau*.

Julech noticed that darker clouds had gathered and the wind had picked up speed. He thought it might rain. He pushed himself to walk faster. He wanted to get at least 15 kilometres of hiking in for the day and didn't want the rain to delay him.

Close to an hour later, the sun had burst through the parting clouds and it appeared that the potential for rain had abated, at least for awhile. The wind had subsided and felt like the temperature had dropped a couple of more degrees. That was alright with Julech and Chippy. They enjoyed hiking with a light cool breeze swishing around them.

*   *   *

Julech slowed his pace and continued to review the different ways to express this notion called love. Earlier he explored how God's eternal love was the source of his own love and the creator of life through love. It now struck him that God's love was not only the source of animate life but also inanimate life. The latter – inanimate life – sounded like a contradiction to him. How could inanimate which meant lifeless be used in conjunction with life?

Julech wasn't much of scientist, but he had learned that scientists considered all matter to have energy in the form of atoms, neutrons and ions, and that energy gave form to matter.

He understood that energy and matter were one, in that one couldn't exist without the other. They were mutually inclusive. Energy moved, morphed, expanded, contracted and exuded life-like qualities within inanimate objects, hence he coined the concept of inanimate life.

He read that biologists, anthropologists and physiologist postulated that 'energy-releasing' reactions were at the core of the living process of all organisms. They were bioenergetic reactions and had continually followed in sequence since the first single-celled organism appeared on earth some 3.5 billion years ago.

He understood that energy was produced through the process of photosynthesis and the breakdown of sugar and that all living things needed energy to work. Humans needed energy to do the simplistic and the most complex of tasks. Animals and insects needed energy to move about. Plants needed energy to grow.

He also heard that scientists theorized that energy had no beginning and end. It just existed. Some went as far as equating energy with God, and stating God was energy, or energy was God.

Julech's mind-monkeys were having a field day as they threw into the mix the energy forces found in the science of thermodynamics, radiation, quantum physics, chemistry and electricity.

When he thought about all those energy sources and gyrations they seemed to have one common element, a cause and effect relationship.

Julech puzzled over this and wondered how causal relationships played into the equation. Everything he knew about how things worked in this world had a cause and effect relationship. So, for energy to exist, even in its most infinitesimal particle it must have had some cause or a source of some form.

"Now, how does this relate to God as source?" he puzzled.

For Julech source was about beginnings, origins or starting points and thus in its definition had causal elements. He determined earlier that this source was God who created everything through love. He now postulated that this God-Source could also 'be at rest' like inactive energy. And, that this inactive energy could still be active in the form of love. Therefore, source could be understood as both the cause of all that exists and at the same time was at the core of all that exists as an indwelling of 'love at rest'.

To equate God only as source as understood as cause, diminished the expansiveness and mind-blowing attributes of an eternal loving God. In simple language, Julech concluded, God was much bigger than source defined as just a starting point for all of creation.

For Julech, God couldn't just be energy, but the source of energy created out of love and remained as indwelling love in all of creation as he knew it. He concluded that this creative and indwelling love-force must have sparked the universe some 14 billion years ago and extended out into an ever-expanding cosmos. Scientists called this sparking of the universe the "Big Bang" theory.

*   *   *

Julech was so caught up in his metaphysical and cosmological mind fields that he forgot to have lunch, and Chippy was now screaming.

"I'm hungry, and besides I need to pee!"

Julech's stomach and bladder agreed with the Chip. He stopped on a grassy knoll and both ran into the bush to relieve themselves.

While Chippy was scrounging around under the underbrush he came upon what was for him a gold mine. There under a large northern red oak tree was a cache of golden brown acorns. It wasn't clear to Chippy how this lonely oak tree had put down its roots in this mountainous region, but it didn't matter. Acorns were one of his favourite foods. He settled down to nature's banquet.

While Julech munched on a bowl of chili, made from mixed dehydrated vegetables and porcubacon, he noticed Chippy running back and forth from the bush to the backpack. He thought it a bit strange, but guessed he was just getting some exercise.

After lunch, Julech laid back to take a quick power nap. As he did so he thought of Catrela. She was often envious of him for his ability to do this. It usually took her over an hour to fall asleep. It didn't matter how hard she tried, she couldn't power nap like Julech. She often said, "I wish I could do that."

In about ten minutes Julech was up and ready to go again. Chippy had curled up on top of the pack. He too was having a nap, but unbeknownst to Julech he was guarding his stash of golden acorns.

When Julech stood, Chippy stretched and instinctively knew it was time to travel again. This time he would follow Julech for awhile rather than ride on the Hat.

The trail levelled off and the two made good progress. It was still cloudy, but the threat of rain had fully subsided. He could see a rainbow some distance away to his left and felt that there was still a strong chance of rain sometime that day.

*   *   *

As he watched the prism of colors emanating from the rainbow his thoughts returned to the various notions of love.

Julech knew he wasn't alone and that God loved him, and through His abundance of love all of creation was born and continued to unfold. God was the embodiment of everything. He was the source of life through love, kept everything in existence for love, and returned everything to Him in eternal love.

"God's fullness of love challenges me to be like Him." he conjectured.

"Just as all created things are an expression of His shared love so too am I called to tap into the love that dwells within me and share it with others."

Julech realized that this is what Jesus must have meant when he said to love God and your neighbor as yourself.

He reasoned, "to love my neighbor as myself is not to appease my 'ego', but to give of myself from my whole being. 'Myself' is about my inner core, an intimacy with who I am, and who I am fully and intimately is connected to the Spirit – the Source within me – and that Spirit is Love personified as I extend myself to others."

For Julech this intimacy was found in the passion of *Eros*, the passionate self-giving of *Agape*, and the natural outpouring of love for one another, known a *Philia*. All three expressions of love were legitimate and wholesome. The passion which was wrapped up in each was one and the same, only expressed differently through one's personhood. They conveyed an outpouring of self to others. And, they were grounded in our humanity with deep connections to our spiritual Source.

Julech learned that through *Eros* men and women became co-partners in God's creation of life; through *Agape* they became co-partners with Him in lighting the fire of love within each other; in *philia* they became the face of God embracing one another with loving kindness.

Julech believed that Agape love was the foundation of Christianity, not righteous religiosity. That love, although simply stated, wasn't always easy.

He knew Jesus said, "A new command I give you: Love one another. As I have loved you, so you must love one another." (John13:34) He also said to love others as oneself, turn the other cheek and love your enemy.

He felt that to love others as one self was hard, to turn the other cheek was harder and to love one's enemy was even harder. So, the path to love wasn't easy.

He was aware that he had often failed in his attempt to love others in the way Jesus commanded.

"The key to falling is getting back up. When I fall out of love, I must get back up and fall back into love," he said to himself in a soft voice.

Julech thought that falling out and falling back into love was a tricky concept to fully appreciate. He remembered Gloria with her two black eyes and battered jaw. Her husband, Jim, had beaten her badly. Their relationship was shattered. Eventually she divorced him but continued to resent him. She found that her resentment ate at her like a cancer and made it difficult for her to form other loving relationships. Over time she came to understand the source of her resentment and his anger. She found it within herself to forgive him. It was a hard journey for her, but it was her way to heal from the inside out and learn to fall back into loving others.

He concluded that there were times when people had to remove themselves from hurtful and abusive situations. Those situations challenged them to search deep within themselves, assess their relationships with others and comprehend the true meaning of love.

Julech was convinced that if Christians really wanted to become a disciple of Jesus then they had to love one another and all of creation. He didn't think that Jesus called his followers to worship him but to become like him and follow his way to a new vision of hope, justice, reconciliation, compassion and peacemaking within a spirit of love.

He looked hard at himself and said, "What I need to do to catch the spirit of Jesus's love is to put myself mindfully and physically within the circle of the poor, marginalized and suffering. That's what Jesus did. So why haven't I done this to the best of my ability. Maybe its because I'm afraid of losing my possessions, what others might say or my own feelings of vulnerability. Unless I move from my comfortable pew to those who aren't in the pew or sit beside those who Jesus sat beside I'm not following his way."

*　　*　　*

With those thoughts percolating within his head he entered a large meadow with a stream flowing into a lake which was nestled up against the Lizard Range. This must be the lake his friends told him about and the place where deer came to rest and drink. It was a gorgeous spot and Julech wanted to spend the night there.

The first thing Julech wanted to do was to jump into the lake and thoroughly wash off four days of dust, sweat and grime. He stripped off his clothes and ran into the water. It was cool, refreshing and welcoming.

Chippy looked at Julech with puzzled eyes. He flopped down on his stomach, stretched out his legs and arms, and asked himself in Chipmunkese, "Should I venture into the water?"

Chipmunks were known to swim, but where Chippy came from there wasn't a pool of water big enough to try out his swimming skills.

"Oh, what the heck, Julech is having fun in there, so here I go!" And with that Chippy dipped his toes into the water and then jumped in whole heartedly.

"By golly, I can swim!" he squealed, and swam out to Julech. He climbed up on Julech's back and when Julech stood up to get out of the water he moved to his shoulder then to the top of his head.

"I wonder what Catrela would say if she saw me now, butt naked walking out of a lake with a chipmunk on my head." The thought made Julech laugh.

Julech quickly dried himself off, built a fire, and planned a meal.

As he put his hand into the pack to gather supplies for his meal, he found Chippy's stash of acorns. Now he knew why his little friend was running back and forth from the bush to the pack during their last stop.

While he lifted out a few acorns to look at them, he heard a stern chipmunkese warning, "Leave those alone, they're mine!"

After they had supped they sat back and relaxed.

The campfire embers glowed while Julech sipped his coffee and took in the stunning sights before him. It was time to review his day.

It started out cool and remained that way for most of the day. It hadn't rained but the potential was there evidenced by a far distant rainbow. They had made good progress with the help of the weather and the hovering goshawk. Chippy had scrounged for his own food and stashed some of it away for another day.

His mediations brought him to a place where he felt he had a deeper understanding of his God as Love and that everything that existed drew meaning from that love.

He was in awe of the complexities of an ever-expanding universe thrusting with energy. He determined there was an interconnectedness, a unifying Source that brought everything together. Everything was bound up in the One. He kept coming back to a realization that God is the embodiment of everything, the beginning of life through love, keeping everything in existence for love, and returning everything to Him in eternal love.

Julech wrapped himself in his bag, and Chippy crawled into the pack.

And so, ended the fourth day.

Becoming Fully Alive

It was 5:45 AM. Julech woke up to the sun lifting from the East under a bevy of clouds, forming a beautiful orange hew with silver linings.

Julech climbed out of the sack.

"Red sky in the morning, a sailors warning."

Chippy didn't stir. He slept with one arm around his acorns. Unlike squirrels who had found their home high up in the hollow of a tree, chipmunks were critters who built their homes underground. Chippy was quite comfortable in his sack-nest. It reminded him of home.

Julech looked over to the lake and sat in awe. There was a family of deer. A large buck, a doe, and a spotted fawn drinking water and eating soft shoots of grass.

The buck heard Julech rise from his sleeping bag and had picked up his scent. It turned and looked at Julech.

The buck grunted to his family as if to say, "Do not be afraid, that fellow doesn't look dangerous." None the less the doe softly grunted to the fawn, "Come closer." Now all three turned their heads and peered at Julech.

Julech sat still and watched. Not sensing danger, the deer went back to their drinking and eating. Soon they wandered off to the long side of the lake, settled down, and kept an eye on their new visitors.

"What a peaceful and wholesome place," Julech said to Chippy.

Chippy opened one eye, crocked his eyebrow and chipped, "uh-huh."

*　　*　　*

As he watched the deer his mind returned to his mediations about the creation story, how everything was created out of love and how love bound the expansiveness and complexity of everything into simple unity.

The deer lived peacefully within the simplicity of the pristine environment in which he found himself. The scene touched him deeply. His feelings were not born out of sentimentality but out of a profound appreciation of the magnitude of love as expressed in this piece of creation.

As he meditated on the majesty of it all, tears rolled down his cheeks and he opened his heart in praise and thanksgiving for what he had just experienced. And, within that frame he chanted *Maranatha.*

*　　*　　*

Leave it to Chippy to wake him out of his silent prayer. Chippy sensed that it was about to rain, and he wanted breakfast before it did.

As Julech refocused on the world around him he too smelled the prospect of rain.

He quickly lit a fire, boiled water and made a pot of porridge. Chippy chewed on his acorns and gulped down a tablespoon of dry oatmeal.

Thunder blasted through the peaceful setting. Rain was swiftly approaching. He looked around and saw that the family of deer had moved to a thick wooded area. He looked for Chippy. He was already in the backpack.

He went into the pack, pushed Chippy aside, and pulled out the tarp and a sheet of clear plastic. He moved quickly to gather two sturdy poles to hold up the tarp and began to assemble a lean-to.

He placed heavy rocks onto the back-side of the tarp, lifted the other side onto the poles with the opening facing opposite the in-coming rain, but still looking out toward the lake. He then stationed the sides with more heavy stones and placed the sheet of plastic on the ground in such a way that he could pull up one end to further shelter both himself and Chippy. He moved all the camping gear and pack into the lean-to. He crawled into his new dwelling place just as the rain came splashing down.

The clouds were heavy, thunder roared, and lightning flashed across the sky. Julech looked up and as far as his eyes could see there were more clouds and rain.

"We're socked in," he shouted, "and, I think we will be here for the day. We might as well get comfy."

With that, he put the pack under his head and leaned back.

Chippy looked at him as if to say, "I'm comfy." He had curled up on Julech's chest and squinted through the plastic sheeting which was half-way up the front of the lean-to.

The lean-to was small and cozy. He stretched out his legs until they touched the plastic sheeting. He watched the rain splash down onto the ground. It was a steady stream of droning droplets that relaxed him. He fell asleep.

When he opened his eyes from his slumber he looked around. He was thankful the rain hadn't penetrated the lean-to. Both he and Chippy were dry. Chippy was still asleep on his chest. It was the downpour that had shaken Julech from his nap.

The rain had the oddest sound as it pelted down on top of the tarp. It seemed soothing and rhythmic yet unnerving and frantic. The music it had played appeared to be a synchronized version of soft, harmonious jazz and jarring punk rock. It was a piece of contradictory noise as far as Julech was concerned.

Fortunately, the cacophony of the rain subsided and gradually the music score went into a more peaceful and melodic pitter patter as it hit the tarp and ground.

Julech studied the scene in front of him. He traced his thoughts back to when he was preparing for his hike and learned about how the trail had become a trail. He sensed Indigenous hunters may have ended up at this spot. It was a perfect resting place and watering hole for deer, elk and moose.

He understood that Indigenous people had a deep respect and spirituality for the land and the animals that inhabited it. They too experienced the interconnectedness of all things and the interdependence of people and other forms of life.

Julech thought that this deep spiritual wisdom had come from centuries of living in concert with nature under the skies of the "Great Spirit" and the natural beauty of the land that had surrounded them. For it to survive, it had to be passed on from generation to generation by spiritual leaders within their communities. Through time, he surmised, it became ingrained within the Indigenous culture and formed their world view. Julech felt that these people of the land joined other ancients found in all corners of the world who came to know the oneness and beauty of the universe.

Indigenous people called the land "Mother Earth." She gave birth to and sustained all life and provided food, water, medicines, clothing and material for their homes. Their deep connection to "Mother Earth" was in keeping with the Spirit that lived in all things, which prompted them to respect and take care of her and all her children. They listened to her heart beat.

That is why, Julech supposed, he heard so much from First Nations people to care for the land. They understood intellectually, emotionally and spiritually that humans were the keepers of the land and must protect it for future generations. It wasn't about the living adults but about their children and their children's children.

In considering these things Julech wondered about the people who had hunted deer at the lake. He sensed their respect for the animals as a source of food and clothing meant that they would only put down what was necessary for them and their village. He saw them in his mind's eye paying homage and thanksgiving for those slain deer and those still alive.

He thought this living in harmony with nature and respect for its bountifulness, could not have prepared North America's first people for the rape and carnage of "Mother Earth" in the years that followed the coming of the settlers from the far-off land. He became sad when he considered how these new people slaughtered wild animals and birds for sport. He thought of those who killed male deer for their antlers rather than for needed sustenance and clothing and hunted ducks and geese for sheer sport.

"What a far cry from the respect they are due as children of 'Mother Earth' gifted to us from the Great Spirit of all life," Julech said to Chippy.

He looked at Chippy with a new-found appreciation and respect.

Chippy yawned, blinked and chipped once again, "I'm alright with God." Then closed his eyes and went back to sleep.

Julech thought of Catrela and her love of gardening and all the critters who came to visit her as she filled the spaces between the shrubs with flowers. He visualized her conversing with her pets, how they listened to her and how they patiently sat beside her as she tended her plants. She had found peace and often said that she was spiritually connected with all that was around her and in that natural space she found a closeness to someone beyond her. Like Chippy, she was saying, "I'm alright with God."

Julech stepped outside of the lean-to. The storm had petered to a misty spray, but the clouds were still heavy with water. The fog was beginning to drift to the upper half of the mountainous range. He felt that the coming hour would see a break in the weather. He went back inside of the lean-to and had another snooze beside his buddy.

Sounds of chewing shattered his peaceful sleep. Chippy was into his acorns. He ate with the intention of arousing Julech. He chewed loudly and threw acorn shells at the walls of the lean-to.

"What are you doing?" laughed Julech.

Chippy just chipped a chuckle.

The sun peeked through the clouds as they parted slightly to show a sliver of blue. It still looked and felt like more rain was on the way.

Julech felt he had about an hour before the next storm would arrive.

Before the first storm hit he had limited time to gather a couple of handfuls of dry grass, twigs and an armful of dead branches. He pulled them out from under the plastic where he had placed them to keep them dry.

He lit a fire.

In no time it was blazing and warming Julech and Chippy from the damp weather; more importantly it was heating itself up so that he could cook a meal.

Julech didn't think the break in the weather was going to last long, so he made something fast. He quickly stirred powdered eggs, milk, flour, a sprinkle of salt and a tablespoon of baking powder. Pancakes, coffee, porcubacon and a few vitamin pills were on the menu. He had brought several 6 ml jars of condiments. Two were filled with maple syrup, and one of them was going to be empty by the end of this meal.

A second wave of thunder rolled in, lightening flashed, the winds picked up and sheets of rain pounded the lean-to. The winds were stronger this time round. Julech watched the poles sway back and forth and worried whether they would weather the storm. He stretched out his arms and held them in place. He alternated between holding and resting for about an hour.

Finally, the winds subsided. The lien-to held. Chippy cuddled up to Julech and both looked out onto the lake shimmering with thousands of jiggling rain-drop ripples.

*   *   *

Julech was mesmerized by the quiet forest rain and the symphony of birds twittering, loons crying out their eerie wailing calls, crickets cricketing, bull frogs croaking and Chippy chipping. They were the sounds of beautiful noise inviting Julech to listen to nature's voices in the tranquility of the late afternoon.

He couldn't help but think of the preceding nights when he looked up into the galaxy of stars, twinkling, shooting, forming, burning, dying, co-mingling and dancing and realized he was just a speck within the ever-expanding cosmos. A truly humbling experience.

The beauty of the nights and rejuvenating rains of the day were for Julech a coming together of nature, spirit and his own humanity. The experience further affirmed for him the oneness of God's infusion of love within all of creation.

God's creation was indeed good, and it required his sincerest respect and faithful stewardship.

He was beginning to understand the bearded man's suggestion, "Listen deeper."

The mellow drippings from the sky along with the quiet chants of the forest wind pushed Julech further into has reverie. He began to think about religion, nature and spirituality.

To some extent religion rankled Julech. He reflected on his own Christian background. Over the centuries Christian religious leaders had developed a prescription of rules, codes and rubrics, that trapped their followers into a box rather than freeing them to embrace the joyous revelation of the Great Spirit that dwelled within them, through them to others and within nature itself.

Julech began to dig deeper.

It appeared to him that many clerical leaders grew to defend their way to God rather than enlightening their followers to open themselves to journey toward the glorious love of God. To defend their way, they sold guilt, sin, and tight rules around rubric based on paternalistic power, order and control. In doing so, they lost the deep mystical path their founder forged when he told his disciples that he was the way, the truth and the life (John 14:6). They concentrated on the path rather than the journey and became religious police rather than spiritual guides.

The way to God, Julech thought, should be one where church leaders encouraged and nurtured the soul to love others and all that was created. Not one where they berated the faithful about sin, guilt and minutiae. The difference for Julech was a God who embraced all in love rather than one who constantly passed judgement and kept score to get even. One way was accepting rather than excluding, unifying rather than dividing, and embracing rather than discriminating.

Julech didn't want to throw out religious practice as something unworthy. He wanted to refocus it away from self-righteous religiosity and dualistic thinking to embracing the freedom of the Spirit. He felt religious leaders should be spiritual leaders and healers. They needed to use the frame of rubric, instruction and guidance as a window to the Holy found within each person and their relation to each other and to everything that existed.

For Julech religious ritual celebration was rich in tradition, culture and meaning.

He said under his breath, "The expression of ritual, liturgy and rubric should be a celebration of joy and exuberance, after all we are celebrating God's love within us and within all. We are celebrating *Agape love.*"

He felt that when religious leaders focused only on the peripherals, whether they be buildings or dictating how people should stand, sit or fold their hands they began to lose their way. Their approach was one of benevolent paternalism designed to keep adults as children.

Yes, Julech thought, children must be taught right from wrong and develop moral certitude which may be found in a code of religious belief, but they should not be treated as children when they become adults. The structures of religious belief, if they were true, provided a framework for spiritual growth. As children grew into adulthood they needed to be encouraged to take on new vistas of spirituality and not afraid to question and touch the Divine within themselves.

It occurred to him that Saint Paul alluded to this when he said,

> "When I was a child, I talked like a child, I thought
> like a child, I reasoned like a child. When I became
> a man, I put the ways of childhood behind me.
> For now we see only a reflection as in a mirror;
> then we shall see face to face. Now I know in part;
> then I shall know full, even as I am fully known.
> (I Cor 13:11-12)

When Julech regarded these things, he referenced the Benedictine Monastery. He thought the Benedictines through their common rule of Peace, Prayer and Work (*Pax, Ora et Labora*) merged the lines between religiosity and spirituality.

The Monastery life he experienced was a place of peace where prayer and work became a way of spiritual living within community. It had structure, organization and rule which was enhanced through prayer and work. The monks' dedication to the divine office and their reverential participation in the sacramental liturgy formed the basis for their prayer and contemplation which they carried out in their work, their relationship with others and with nature.

At The Abbey the Benedictine fathers and brothers work entailed teaching, cooking, farm labour, masonry, grounds keeping, art, music, leading retreats and advising on spiritual matters. This varied work was complemented with the prayer of the hours, *Lectio Divina* and liturgical celebration.

"It occurs to me, Chippy, that this co-mingling of peaceful prayer, contemplation and work within smaller communities might be a model for reducing religiosity while strengthening spirituality," Julech said.

"Maybe."

*　　*　　*

Chippy was jumping up and down, talking a blue streak in chipmunkese and scratching at the clear plastic window. The storm had passed. It was sunny outside and time to run in the meadow and find something interesting. Julech couldn't agree more. It was time to stretch his legs and do some exploring himself.

Julech walked over to the lake, surveyed it and saw a creek flowing into the waters on the north westerly side. His knowledge of fishing told him that where streams join lakes fish are not far behind. He hiked alongside the lake's edge to the mouth of the stream. The rain had encouraged insects to come out of their hiding places and flit about. There were dragonflies, mayflies, damselflies, water striders, mosquitoes, craneflies and midges. All a feast for the brook trout frequenting the lake and stream.

Julech watched as the trout jumped out of the water to feed on the flies. That was all he needed to know. He high-tailed it back to camp, hacked off a nice straight flexible willow branch, grabbed his fish hooks and line, and headed as fast as he could back to the mouth of the creek. In a few minutes he had a handful of flying insects. He was going fly fishing and fresh fish was on his menu.

The fish were hungry. They had laid low in the waters during the storm and when it passed they instinctively knew that there would be a cornucopia of flies to quell their hunger. A few of those flies were on a line tied at the end of Julech's make-shift fishing pole.

Julech was lucky. Within twenty minutes three nice speckled brook trout had found his flies. One by one they were quickly drawn onto the shoreline and readied for the frying pan.

He was a happy camper and whistled all the way back to the lean-to. He hadn't felt this good since he had caught his first fish back in the headwaters of the Elk river.

Brook trout, seasoned black beans, rice topped with nuts and a biscuit rounded out the menu. Soon a crackling fire broke the silence of the late afternoon. Chippy smelled the smoke from the fire and knew something was cooking. He was ready to eat.

He bounced into camp, looked at the pan on the fire, smelled the beans and rice.

"Fish? Ugh!"

Julech was ready this time. He had found out a couple of days earlier that Chippy didn't like fish, so he prepared a dish of nuts, dried fruit, tree fungi, and a dash of crushed acorns.

"Now that's a delicious looking dish!" Chippy blurted out with glee.

They settled down to their meal with a tinge of hunger written on their faces. After they had supped they sat back. They were filled, relaxed and contented.

Chippy, in Chipmunkese chipped, "Yes, that was delicious!"

Julech, in English said "Ditto!"

Julech nursed a cup of cocoa and watched the sun fade behind the mountain. He was honored one more time by the family of deer as they came back to the lake for one last drink before bedding down.

The clouds that cried for most of the day had disappeared but left a damp and cool evening. He sat in the shelter and gazed into the glow of the embers and reviewed the last five days of hiking on what he now called *The Old Deer Trail.*

*   *   *

All is created out of love in the image of Love. I am called to grow into Love's likeness by sharing that love with others. This creative force I call God, Yahweh, Abba, Father, Mother, Holy, Divine, and Good. God graces Himself within me and all of creation. She holds all in existence through the power of her Spirit. He is found and celebrated in the tiniest of particles to the expanse of the universe. In silence I hear Him and in everything I see Her.

In sequential time I have come to know God. The unfolding of my understanding of the ebb and flow of the universe and all that exists unpacks my understanding of the Divine. The God of 'no time' is revealed to me 'in time'. The evolutionary process of knowing the unknown leads me ever deeper into the Love of the eternal unknown.

I see God in the face of another. The other and all that exists is infused with His love. His outpouring of Love is manifested by the infinitesimal spark of energy and the enormity of an expanding universe. When I listen and look deeply my hidden God is found and the Almighty is revealed. I can never be alone.

Julech recited a stanza from another poem, *The Kingdom of God is Within You*, by Francis Thompson.

> O world invisible, we view thee,
> O world intangible, we touch thee,
> O world unknowable, we know thee,
> Inapprehensible, we clutch thee!

Julech sensed that we lived in a time where there is a blending of wisdom, religion and science. *The ancients understood the Almighty as the indwelling source of life, nature and the cosmos. Religion in its purest form opens the doors to the revelation of the Divine and draws us to worship the inexpressible. Science discovers the data to substantiate and inform us about our spiritual Source. The three come together in a fusion of spirituality uncovering the simplicity of unity where all is one and one is all.*

"It's time," Julech said to himself, "that we put away all religious and scientific polarization, discrimination and divisiveness and open ourselves to embrace the deep spirituality that binds them together."

Julech felt 'fully alive' and wondered how he could become the face of love in his relationships with others and the world around him. He looked forward to the morning and the next stretch of his journey and the surprises that were in store for him.

He let the fire burn out and crawled into his sleeping bag. Chippy settled into his nest. Both closed their eyes and rested in the love and beauty that surrounded them.

And so, ended the fifth day.

Born to Serve with Love

"Start by doing what is necessary
Then what is possible, and suddenly
You are doing the impossible"
St. Francis of Assisi

Julech Unravels Compassion

Dawn opened the sky to the beginning of a beautiful morning. The thunder, lightning, winds, and heavy rain had long passed. Day six was shaping up to be another great day for hiking.

Julech and Chippy woke to the grunts of the deer as they passed the lean-to on their way to the lake. There they had their early morning drink and munched on the new shoots of grass and leaves. Julech was once again moved. The peaceful scene provided him with the space to begin his morning meditation.

He remembered having a conversation with a gentleman he met in Starbucks back home. During the conversation he learned that his name was Peter. Pete for short. They were talking about the image of God as the source of all of creation. Julech asked him what his image of God looked like. Pete placed his hands to his face and said, "Like this." Julech wasn't sure whether Pete knew the significance of what he just said and did, but it left a profound impression on him. He interpreted Pete's gesture as, "I am made in the image of God, and I project that image outward to others in love."

As a Christian, Julech came to know Jesus as God incarnate, born in time as man and as 'the Christ' existing beyond time as eternal Divinity. The Man/Christ was one and the same.

> *The Jesus of Nazareth as man opened a new way to touching God through love, forgiveness and compassion. Jesus as 'the Christ' is the 'Son of God' born of the Father and rooted within the Father as creator and source in oneness with the Father. The Father and Son are indivisible and exist in unity, flowing one from the other in Love, which Christians call the Spirit. The three are called the one Triune God with no beginning and no end. They, as One, embody the flowing of love to one another and an outpouring of love to all that exists.*

It was this outflowing of love to one another that Julech saw as the kernel for his future meditations. In this frame he opened his heart and mind and repeated his mantra *Maranatha.*

*　　*　　*

Chippy screeched his morning alarm, "Hey, its time to eat."

Julech smiled, "What a life, all you do is sleep, eat, run around and get carried about."

"Not a bad life," came the chipped reply.

He appreciated the little rascal though and hoped Chippy stayed with him for the rest of the hike.

Julech prepared a hearty breakfast which included a vegetable and egg omelet, a side order of mush, left over biscuits and of course a cup of strong coffee. He supplemented Chippy's acorns with dry apricots, a piece of biscuit and watered-down coffee.

Julech looked forward to continuing his hike up the trail but had misgivings about leaving the solitude of the lake and its picturesque scene of field flowers, deer and flying insects.

He slipped on his pack. Chippy, now familiar with the routine, ran up his arm and perched himself on top of the *Chapeau*.

They were off, but not before Julech looked back at the lake and deer one more time.

They went around a large bend and headed north, hugging the east side of Fernie Ridge. On his left he saw another range of the Rocky Mountains.

As the trail began to undulate in almost wave fashion, Julech was taken with the sounds of birds. He heard blue jays, goldfinches, nuthatches and thrashers. He questioned what thrashers were doing so high up in the Rockies but paid no heed to his query. He just listened to their cricket-like songs.

Chippy liked the bird songs so much that they had lulled him to sleep. Julech couldn't figure out how this little chipmunk could balance himself on top of his *Chapeau* while asleep. It didn't matter how he did it. Chippy was asleep and Julech was enjoying the sites and sounds of the trail. As he trudged along and listened to the sounds of nature he decided to call the remaining trail home "The Black Gold Trail".

*   *   *

For the next hour Julech mulled over his earlier meditation on extending love to others. He reflected on the practice of compassion and the parable of the Good Samaritan as told in Luke 10:25-37.

Jesus told a parable about a traveler who had been robbed, stripped of clothing, beaten and left on the roadside. First a priest and then a Levite came by, however they had paid no attention to the man. Finally, a Samaritan helped the traveler. He had bound his wounds, brought him to a nearby Inn and paid for his room. This was a telling story because those who had passed him by were regarded as stalwart citizens, whereas Samaritans were generally despised. Jesus told this story in response to a question from a lawyer, "And who is my neighbor?"

For Julech the story uncovered a natural principle: that compassion was rooted in humanity, and that he shouldn't let prejudice, differences or discrimination blind him when people were hurting. Everyone was worthy of compassion.

Julech considered his meditations from the past few days. He now felt that the principle of compassion should be extended to all living things, the natural world that surrounded him and the whole of the expanding cosmos.

"Maybe I should unpack this whole concept and consider it from different angles," he said to himself.

"Are you with me on that, Chippy?"

Chippy stirred on the Hat when he heard his name, but he was more into sleep than listening to Julech.

Julech thought a good place to start was to clarify the word 'compassion' and see where that would take him.

> Compassion invokes concern for the suffering or misfortunes of others. Its meaning is simple yet complex. It is like a crystal reflecting over fourteen synonyms including: empathy, care, concern, solicitude, sensitivity, warmth, love, tenderness,

mercy, leniency, tolerance, kindness, humanity, and charity.

Compassion literally means "to suffer together." It relates to a feeling that arises when one is confronted with another's suffering and becomes motivated to relieve that suffering.

In Julech's mind compassion shouldn't be dismissed as a "touchy feely" phenomenon. He knew recent scientific research had uncovered anthropological, biological and a physiological basis for it.

He understood that the practice of compassion might have been necessary for human survival. It had been hypothesized that early ancestors needed to act compassionately to keep their clan together. He couldn't quite fathom how cave people exhibited compassion but thought the harsh conditions under which they lived might have had something to do with it.

He had read stories about saints and sinners alike who acted with compassion during times of plagues, fractious wars and atrocities of the past. He thought of present day institutions which he took for granted such as hospitals, education and emergency services that often grew out of those same plagues, wars and atrocities. They were founded by committed and compassionate people.

He learned that physiological changes took place when people felt compassion. Their heart rate slowed down, they secreted the bonding hormone oxytocin, and when they experienced the suffering of others certain parts of their brain lit up which often resulted in wanting to approach and care for them.

When he compared compassion to empathy he found a relationship between the concepts, but they were not necessarily the same. Empathy was a more general term and referred to people's ability to both walk in the perspective of and the feel of emotions of another person; compassion included those feelings and motivated people to help the other. Each flowed from the other, but people could exhibit one without the other.

Julech stopped for a few moments, pulled out his phone, and googled the word compassion. He found hundreds of quotes that spanned time, philosophies, religions and cultures. He highlighted these few:

- "Be kind, for everyone you meet is fighting a harder battle." Plato
- "Compassion is a muscle that gets stronger with use." Mahatma Gandhi
- "If we have no peace, it is because we have forgotten that we belong to each other." Mother Teresa
- "Love and compassion are necessities, not luxuries. Without them, humanity cannot survive." The Dalai Lama
- "Wisdom, compassion, and courage are the three universally recognized moral qualities of men." Confucius.

No doubt, Julech thought, that believers of different faiths had a compassionate outreach. And people with no affiliation with any religion, some who claimed to be atheists, contributed to humanitarian causes in compelling and compassionate ways.

Julech considered his own faith community. Christians had often recited the gospel story about the Good Samaritan as an example of compassionate care. However, that story didn't necessarily set them apart as there were countless other cultures where similar stories were told.

They also had quoted the golden rule: "Treat others as you would like to be treated", or, "Love your neighbor as yourself". Those teachings were not good enough either as similar admonitions were posed in ancient and modern literature by many non-Christians.

He mulled over the companies and organizations he knew where people had exhibited a form of compassion. They supported community needs by fostering food drives, raising funds for the mentally or physically challenged or treating others within their places of work with genuine respect and empathy.

He observed that governments acted with a sense of compassion when they established policies that led to the care of others in the fields of health, education and housing and in times of crises such as when natural disasters hit.

Finally he thought of all the not-for-profit community-based agencies that acted out of a compassionate outreach. Many hadn't any religious affiliation. Those that spear headed them may have had a religious background but the agencies themselves were non-partisan and non-religious.

He concluded that people from various walks of life, different cultures, philosophies and faith had throughout history viewed compassion as a fundamental value for purposeful living. And now there was neurological evidence which localized the practice of compassion within the brain. Generally, people cared. That gave enough proof for Julech that compassion was rooted in humanity.

Julech turned all this over in his mind and posed the question, "Was the approach to compassion profoundly similar in all major religions or was it different?"

Just as he was about to focus on that question, there was a loud chipping sound and pounding of feet emanating from the top of his head. Chippy was in a chipmunkese snit.

*   *   *

Chippy had an uncanny knack of sensing danger, sniffing the air for potential predators and seeing things in the distance that might harm him. This time all three antenna went up.

There in a distance Julech saw a huge black bear in front of a blueberry patch. It had smelled and heard the on-coming travelers. It was standing straight up on its hind legs with its front paws hanging downward and was looking directly at them.

"Thank goodness, it's not a grizzly," whispered Julech.

"What's a grizzly?" quizzed Chippy.

"Grizzlies are more aggressive than black bears."

"Oh. I thought all bears were the same."

Julech knew that black bears were predictable, normally shy and retiring. They usually avoided humans unless their food supply was threatened. They were also sociable and prone to sharing their space. When they were threatened or frightened they often ran away or climbed a tree.

"However, they are unbelievably strong and not to be tangled with," Julech said to Chippy.

"I know," came the quick reply

Julech sized up the situation. The berry patch seemed large enough for the bear to share. There were no cubs around, so it needn't take evasive action. And, the bear appeared to be standing on its hind legs out of curiosity rather than of hostility.

He knew black bears were not territorial. He looked around and couldn't see any more and heaved a sigh of relief.

As Julech and Chippy approached the blueberry patch, Blackie (Julech's nick name for the bear) kept standing at attention.

The two hikers stopped at the far side of the patch. Blackie sensed that things would be alright, sat down and continued filling his belly with berries.

The blueberry patch was a good place to take a break. So, with one eye on Blackie Julech lowered his pack, let Chippy off his shoulder, and settled down for a feast of blueberries.

"We're just going to eat blueberries and that's it for lunch," he said to Chippy.

"No nuts and nothing more?"

"That's right. I don't want Blackie to smell our food in case he wanted it rather than the blueberries in front of him."

"That's a good plan."

Julech filled a plastic bag with blueberries and shoved them into his backpack. The two left the scene with Blackie still gorging himself with berries. He wasn't troubled with the hikers leaving.

Julech made sure he kept his distance from Blackie as they moved beyond the patch.

"I better keep my eye out for other bears," Julech said, "and, I better be careful at night in case they want to visit us and my backpack."

About 30 minutes after leaving the patch, Julech returned to his musings about compassion.

*　　*　　*

He understood that compassion was a key value for Christianity, Islam, Buddhism and Judaism and other western and eastern spiritual traditions. The expression of compassion appeared to be profoundly similar in all religions and spiritual traditions but was it profoundly the same? He thought that compassion from a humanistic perspective might be the same, but how it was integrated within the various belief systems might differ.

Julech posed the question another way: "What makes Christian compassion different than the compassion shown by others in our world? What was it about compassion that sets the Christian message apart? Or, was there any difference?"

He knew that three of the major religions, Christianity, Islam and Judaism believed in the same God. Perhaps, he thought that's where common ground might be found.

Julech reasoned "Compassion is rooted in love and God is love. It seems then whenever people show compassion we witness the 'hand' of God's love. People of all walks of life, believers and non-believers of whatever persuasion participate in that love whether they recognize it or not."

As Julech pondered this, he posed another question.

"Is there a God, or a Supreme Loving Being beyond our collective ego?"

For the past several days he had been meditating on the image, likeness and love of God. Now, he was exploring compassion as an expression of that love.

"What the heck," he said out loud, "now I come up with a 'big but' – but is there a God?"

Religious and spiritual leaders, scientists and billions of people past and present had believed in something or someone beyond themselves. He had explored the creation story, the indwelling of love throughout the cosmos in the first leg of his journey, and only now he posed the question: "Is there a God to begin with?"

He looked around at the expanse of the mountain ranges and the natural beauty that was unfolding before him. He invoked the mystics and wisdom people from centuries past and the present love-comfort within him – all led him to believe that there was indeed a God. But this wasn't scientific proof, he realized, maybe it's just some mental gymnastics soothing his ego. Atheists would say that's what was happening.

Julech remembered that brain evidence regarding consciousness and spirituality, hadn't scientifically proved the existence of God one way or the other. Things happened within a brain when people meditated but that didn't necessarily prove that there was a God. Nor could atheists disprove God. They could deny God, but they couldn't disprove Him. In that sense atheism was predicated on a believe system as well.

"So, we humans have a choice and my choice is to go with God. I believe that has a much greater chance for hope, love and compassion."

Julech believed the evidence for that statement revealed itself when he considered the magnitude of the universe and those who were a force for good in this world.

"Without my fully knowing," he said to himself, "I suggest the evidence will point to those who believe in a higher power than themselves have greater staying power as a force for good than those who don't."

With that, Julech turned back to the questions he posed earlier, "What makes Christian compassion different than the compassion shown by others? What is it about compassion that set the Christian message apart? Or, was there any difference?"

He recognized the starting point for understanding compassion was found in love as taught by all religions and spiritual wisdom. It seemed to him that compassion then mirrored a world view that grew out of one's religious and spiritual roots.

Julech's world view was formed in Christian faith, or belief. Without commitment to the teachings of Jesus and growing in the understanding of the cosmic Christ there was no difference in how Christians demonstrated compassion.

For Julech, compassion must be connected to living fully in Christ and that living in Christ must continue to unfold in relation to others and the world around him. He considered this unfolding as a continual process and that he too remained a work in progress.

From Julech's perspective it was simple: Christian compassion was rooted in Christ and found in faith and hope.

If Christian compassion wasn't Christ-centered, then the expression of compassion by Christians was the same as non-Christians. There was no difference. It remained wholly humanistic.

Julech whispered under his breath. "Gees, I'm not trying to raise Christian compassion above other forms of compassion or promote "a holier than thou" attitude. If I did, I would be guilty of demeaning the very meaning of Christian compassion. I think what I'm trying to postulate is that when Christians speak about compassion from their perspective they can't leave out Christ. They must clothe themselves with Christ in very concrete ways."

Julech was finding so much excitement in exploring this concept that he forgot to take in the beauty that surrounded him.

Besides his legs were getting tired so it was time to sit and take a break.

*   *   *

He took out his water canister, a protein bar and a handful of blueberries from his pack and shared them with Chippy.

Chippy had been quiet for the past hour and a half and now wanted to run around the rocks. When he saw the nuts and berries he stuck by Julech until they were all gone. After that he took off to explore the area.

Julech looked out to the west and saw range after range of mountains. The hikers were higher up on the east side of the Fernie Range, but it was still hot and there were fewer tall trees to shade them. Some of the mountain peaks had snow on them. They looked like glaciers. Secretly, he hoped to come across a glacier before he ended his journey.

He looked at the colorful orange and green lichens, mosses and liverworts hugging the rocks. Further in the distance clusters of creamy white and blue mountain lupines, lavender pasque flowers, blue bells of Scotland and bright rose-colored moss campions caught his eye.

As he had looked at the flowers and scenery in front of him, he decided to snap a bit of mountainous charm on his phone camera to take back to Catrela.

He turned and saw water trickling out from under the rocks. He was grateful for the streams that flowed down from the mountain tops. They had gifted him with fresh water to replenish his canister on a regular basis. He had to drink about a liter of water every 90 minutes or so to keep his fluids and electrolytes in balance. On extremely hot days he added a salt pill and some dried dates to keep his potassium in check.

Julech glanced at his watch and planned for another hour of hiking before breaking for the night. It was time to move on.

While they were sheltered under the lean-to during the storm Julech had taught Chippy to respond to his whistle. He put his fingers to his mouth and gave the sound of "its time to move on!" Chippy came bouncing down the rocks where he had been chewing lichen, hopped on Julech's arm and scampered to his perch.

*　　*　　*

Julech was astounded with the beauty that surrounded him, but he still wanted to explore the link between compassion and Christian teaching. He thought of one of his favorite people, Pope Francis, who consistently urged Christians to become the face of Jesus through compassionate action.

He recalled a story about Corrie ten Boom who was a Christian of the Dutch Reformed Church. Corrie suffered great family and personal loss during the Second World War because her family hid her Jewish brothers and sisters within their home. She and her family had been imprisoned for their crime.

She survived. Unfortunately, many of her family members didn't. After the war Corrie had made it her personal mission to show others how to walk with a compassionate Jesus.

One of the analogies she had used to get her point across was to have Christian's view themselves as a glove and it was Jesus's hand that moved the glove.

As Julech was imagining the analogy of the glove he thought of all those saintly people who dawned the glove. In his catholic tradition he remembered saints who had become his role models for compassionate care. He thought of: Francis Xavier Cabrini, Vincent de Paul, Elizabeth Ann Seton, Teresa of Calcutta, John Bosco, Francis of Assisi and many of the walking saints of his time.

He also envisioned the thousands of compassionate people who were not Christ-centered wearing the glove. Their glove had moved because of the same love of God. It was an invisible hand that moved them. Many didn't recognize the hand, but it was there.

Julech had begun to climb a steep hill and he could see he was getting closer to the top of the ridge. Perhaps, because he was working so hard on his climb and feeling a bit burdened, he wondered if people could feel over stressed in their compassionate giving. To keep with the analogy, "could the glove fit too tightly?"

Julech had met care givers who gave of themselves to such an extent that they burned out with compassionate overload. Often, they experienced high levels of stress which resulted in complaining, guilt, and exhaustion.

He felt strongly that people who cared for others needed to take time out to care for themselves. They required a balance that left room for both self-compassion and other-compassion. Self-compassion was not a selfish act but an important ingredient to conserve energy for other-compassion. He had read that Mother Teresa ensured that her followers took time off to reenergize with prayer and relaxation.

He concluded that whether it was with prayer, relaxation or a vacation it was important for people to break from the pressure of compassionate care. This was especially true for those who provided care in hospitals, long term care facilities and other agencies where extra ordinary demands were placed on them.

*   *   *

Julech and Chippy had arrived at a clearing where they could look directly west at the closing of the day. It was too early for the sun to set, but he anticipated a beautiful evening as he gazed at the snow-capped range of mountains in the distance.

When he was setting up camp another hiker coming from the north joined him. Clancy was his name. Clancy also hiked with a buddy, a gentle sheep dog. Wooly was his name

Initially Chippy was perturbed when he saw Wooly. He immediately hid in the backpack. Woolly wasn't the least bit interested in Chippy. He was curious when Chippy poked his head out of the pack but that was about as far as it went.

Chippy slowly pulled himself out of the pack and kept a wary eye on Woolly. Still no movement from Woolly, who now was resting beside Clancy.

Chippy, ever the explorer, crept closer to Woolly.

Woolly turned, sniffed and then put his head down onto his front paws.

Chippy drew closer.

Woolly didn't move.

Soon Chippy was eye ball to eye ball to Woolly.

Woolly looked at him through the hair in his eyes, twitched his nose and let out a sigh as if to say, "What are you afraid of?"

Woolly was one big cream puff, who obviously wasn't a threat to small animals.

Julech asked Clancy about his unruffled dog.

It turned out that Clancy had cats, gerbils and rabbits back home and Woolly became their friend and protector. On the trail Woolly kept close to him and never once ran after squirrels, rabbits or birds. Woolly just lumbered along and minded his own business.

It didn't take long for Chippy to figure out that Woolly was a good guy. Soon they were lying beside each other.

The two men shared the menu for supper.

Julech had lentils for soup. Clancy threw in some rice.

Clancy had dried beef strips. Julech had potatoes.

Julech added Clancy's dried carrots to his dried peas.

Julech made blueberry biscuits and Clancy prepared a side bowl of wild strawberries.

They both enjoyed what they thought was a well-balanced hiker's meal.

Wooly ate the leftovers from the supper meal, while Chippy chewed on the blueberry biscuit and wild strawberry dessert.

After their meal Woolly and Chippy ventured out to explore their surroundings. It was comical to watch Chippy sitting on top of Woolly's back as Woolly sniffed his way into the underbrush.

Clancy and Julech compared hiking notes. Clancy had been on the trail for five days. He had approached the hike from the eastern side of the town. Both had experienced the storm, other than that the weather had been perfect.

Clancy told Julech that if he took a short detour from the trail, he could climb up to a glacier. That interested Julech and he tucked the route away in his memory bank.

Julech asked him why he was hiking.

Clancy hailed from Australia and came to Canada to hike the Rockies. He landed in Fernie and looked at all the hiking trails and decided on this one because it seemed like a challenge. He was smitten with the grand landscape, the beauty of the sunsets and sunrises and the natural growth that had surrounded him.

Julech shared his intentions about his journey – that it was a journey of self-discovery for him. He ended with the idea that God was hidden but could be found within and around them within the natural world.

The two men had different approaches to the hike. One was taken with what was going on around him, the other with what was going on within him. Both agreed that the beauty of nature could lead to a Power beyond them and that they were just a couple of dots in the great scheme of things.

After their campfire talk, Julech's reflected on his conversation with Clancy and his mind turned to Catrela. She had approached life more at the natural level and he more at the intellectual level.

Catrela loved to immerse her hands in the soil, tend to her flowers, animals and bird friends. Her spirituality was strengthened by her touch with the vitality of the soil. His came more from his readings, meditation and contemplation. She had taught him much about the importance of connecting to "Mother Earth," or "getting real" as she called it. Maybe Catrela's approach to spirituality was more in line with Clancy's than his.

Julech let the fire die down and the four of them looked west as the sun set. It was a beautiful closing of the day. The sun tucked itself behind the mountains leaving a lavender and orange tinge to the sky. Within a short time, it grew dark and a gorgeous display of sparkling stars and a rounded moon graced the sky. All four retired for the night, only this time Chippy slept under the arm of his new furry friend.

As Julech reviewed his day, he felt he gained a deeper understanding of Christian compassion. "I must put on the golden glove of loving compassion more consistently," he said to himself. He then remembered a quote from St. Teresa of Avila:

Christ has no body now on earth but yours,

No hands but yours,

No feet but yours,

Yours are the eyes, through which Christ's compassion is to look out to the earth,

Yours are the feet by which He is to go about doing good,

And yours are the hands by which He is to bless us now.

He closed his eyes and so ended the Sixth Day.

Compassion Leads to Kindness

MORNING SEEMED TO COME TOO SOON FOR THE FOUR SLEEPERS. As usual it was Chippy who had woke up first and sounded the alarm. Woolly lifted his head with a start. He wasn't used to the chipmunkese racket. He woofed and Chippy stepped back in bewilderment and then sat in silence. Woolly snorted, put his head down on his front paws and closed his eyes again.

Julech smiled.

"Well that put you in your place. Next time chip a little quieter. You have guests and it seems like they want to sleep a little longer."

"Not a bad idea," chipped Chippy, and with that he crawled into his corner in the pack.

Julech rolled out of his bag. It was dawn and chilly. Since they were on the east side of the mountain facing west he couldn't feel the warmth of the early morning sun. He put his bag around his shoulders and prepared for his meditative practice.

*   *   *

He wanted to continue where he left off, yesterday. The question today was not "What is compassion?" But, "How do we live compassion in our everyday lives? How do we make the concept concrete?"

Julech estimated that people generally spent a third of their time at work, a third sleeping or resting and the other third or less being active at home or in the community. His experience told him that those hours weren't fixed. They could slide up and down depending on their work and financial resources. Where in that time cycle did people practice compassion? Was compassion something they consciously called upon or was it a natural approach or an ingrained attitude they had as they related to others and the world around them? Did they say, "OK, it's time for compassion", or was it in their bones, so to speak, and came to them without thinking? Or, was it both?

He felt that there were certain times in life when people were called to show genuine compassion, To put on the "glove." Perhaps these were times when compassion came naturally. He thought about his own experiences that called him to show compassion when someone in his family or one of his friends were ill, or he came across an accident on the highway, or encountered a homeless person, or saw a bird with a broken wing. He guessed a person with a compassionate heart could be open to those types of situations with a genuine outpouring of feeling and love. He also thought that there were people who 'hardened' themselves to those situations or didn't know how to respond when they found themselves there.

He wondered about people who had a hard time displaying compassion. It wasn't that they hadn't shown compassion in their own way, it's just that they seemed to have what some termed a "cold heart". They had difficulty in expressing their feelings and often saw things in black and white terms. Sometimes they approached illnesses, death and the needs of others and said, "Well that's life, get over it."

Then there were those who appeared to be highly objective thinkers and had difficulty in getting in touch with their own feelings. They kept their feelings bottled up inside rather than expressing them outwardly. He had met individuals who had tears in their eyes but couldn't verbally express their feelings. Julech thought they had a quiet sense of compassion or a "warm heart" but kept their feelings to themselves.

Julech also felt there were times when it was appropriate not to say anything. He thought of the times when he was called just to sit with an ill individual, give a warm hug, hold a hand or just listen without expressing any words. However, he recognized that some people had difficulty expressing compassion that way.

He concluded that compassion could come naturally for some and could be difficult for others. Each would express it in their own way. As he thought more about it he wondered whether people could be taught how to express compassion or improve their own compassionate outreach.

Perhaps a partial answer to those questions grew out of his musings about how various beliefs, cultural moorings and family values shaped one's view about compassion. He reflected on the centuries of Christian contemplatives and Buddhist teachings about compassion and how they instructed their followers to nurture compassion within themselves and others.

He thought of the various ways of how adults had nurtured compassion within themselves and others. They included: role modeling, storytelling, self-awareness and sensitivity workshops, meditation, incremental steps to compassionate application, personal affirmations, compassionate accountability sessions, animal therapy, how-to-videos, therapeutic group sessions, self-learning, spiritual reading and reflective prayer. Each were important approaches but when taken together they exhibited an impressive body of teaching and learning methods and processes; and, when consistently applied had helped people learn ways to improve their ability to compassionately relate to others.

"Yes," he said to himself, "people could learn to become compassionate and deepen their compassionate outreach, if they were encouraged, nurtured and taught. In short one's ability to develop a compassionate heart requires a willingness for self-introspection and a commitment to change behaviours."

Julech had come to understand that compassion could be learned and expressed in many different ways. It depended on the situation and how comfortable people were in expressing their own feelings and their openness to touch one more facet of God's diamond of love.

He resolved that it wasn't so important to judge whether others were compassionate, but that he continue to grow his compassionate muscle, and know that when he was compassionate it came from a deep sense of spirituality born out of his relationship with his God. St. Paul said it this way:

> "Praise be to the God and Father of our Lord Jesus
> Christ, the Father of compassion and the God of
> all comfort, who comforts us in all our troubles,
> so that we can comfort those in any trouble with
> the comfort we ourselves receive from God."
> (2 Cor.1:3-4)

On that note Julech hummed *Maranatha*.

*　　*　　*

Chippy had enough sleep. He jumped out of the pack and onto Woolly. It was time to get up, eat breakfast and move on.

This time Woolly stood up, shook himself, yawned and went over to Clancy and licked his nose. That did it. Everyone was now up and almost ready for another day. Julech joined the other three and prepared a fire for breakfast.

Julech and Clancy had agreed that pancakes, scrambled eggs, biscuits and strong coffee would make a hearty breakfast.

Woolly wasn't as finicky about eating as Chippy. He scoffed down the leftovers from breakfast. Chippy, on the other hand nibbled on his nuts, took a bite out of a wild strawberry and drank a lid full of cold coffee.

The men rolled up their bags, put out the fire and packed their backpacks. They exchanged e-mail addresses for a future connection and then, with their friends, took off in different directions. Woolly plodded beside Clancy and Chippy sat on top of Julech's *Chapeau.*

Julech followed the path along the ridge of the mountain. It was narrower than previous but comfortable to walk. He noticed that there was heavy shale on each side of the path and began to slow down his gait to view the slabs.

Shale was soft, stratified sedimentary rock that formed from hardened mud or clay. It could easily be split into slabs. Back home Julech surrounded his fish pond and walkway with black and gray shale.

Shale was also known to house fossils.

Julech found it hard to believe that approximately 500 million years ago the Rocky Mountains he was now exploring were under a sea of water. About 350 million years later the waters receded leaving aquatic plants, crustaceans and other arthropods imbedded in the shale as fossils and imprints. He had heard that giant ammonites were found east and north of where he was hiking. The one found on Coal Mountain to the north was one of the largest, if not the largest, in the world.

He didn't expect to find a giant ammonite on the trail. However, neither did the hikers on the Coal Mountain trail.

He said to himself, "Who knows, it might happen."

Julech had greater interest in finding smaller arthropod fossils. He kept a sharp eye on the slabs of shale as he passed by them.

It took about 90 minutes to travel about half of the distance he normally would have traveled in that same time frame. The sun had peeked over the side of the mountain and warmed up the air. He needed a break from the rocky trail, so he stopped to take a rest alongside a cliff overlooking the valley. He looked up the trail and saw that it wasn't as rough as the last few kilometres, so he decided to linger a little longer on the cliff.

Chippy was enjoying himself nibbling on a couple of nuts, supplementing them with some water and moss he uncovered around the shale. He also wanted to explore under shale for some insects and other tidbits. More time for running around suited him just fine.

Julech looked over the valley and focused on his morning meditation.

*   *   *

"How do Christians exhibit compassion in the workplace?" he asked himself.

"First off," Julech answered, "Christians needn't broadcast that they were Christians. They just had to wear the glove and act in a way that exhibited Christian compassion – a compassion that was kind, genial, patient, joyful, humble, forgiving, respectful, tolerant, empathetic and all summed up in the notion of love. If they did that others would notice, and they would set an example for them."

Julech trusted that if people could bring those qualities to the workplace, hope, optimism and goodness would follow. He wanted to help create a positive, up-lifting and an inspiring workplace where people cared for each other and their customers. He felt he could contribute to a compassionate workplace with the attribute called kindness.

For Julech compassion led to kindness, but kindness didn't necessarily lead to compassion. Take his colleague Joe for instance. Joe was a kind individual, but his kindness was devoid of any feeling. He didn't miss an opportunity to say thank you, send a get-well card to a sick friend or a colleague. He saw it as his duty and politeness was the right thing to do. His kindness gave others the sense that he was on auto-pilot. Joe didn't raise his acts of kindness to the level of compassion, where he felt the 'hurt' or 'needs' of the other. Joe's acts of kindness were appreciated by his colleagues and friends, but they couldn't warm up to him. He kept his distance.

Jane, on the other hand, was a compassionate individual. Her compassionate attitude extended to acts of kindness. She did the same things as Joe but in a way that people understood that she was 'walking in their shoes' so to speak. Her kindness came from her heart and people knew it, they could see it in her eyes and demeanor.

Julech felt if he was genuinely kind to others everyone would gain. He wanted to be more like Jane than Joe.

He whispered softly, "Kindness doesn't take much skill. I can just do it! I could do simple acts of kindness such as open a door for another, smile, say thank you, pick up things cluttering the floor, leave a common work room tidy or place a hand over my mouth when I coughed. All these actions were simple acts of *kindness* that were noticed by others. If I didn't do them, they would become *simple acts of unkindness* and people would notice them as well."

He considered the more darker side of *unkindness* which brewed inside work places such as those repeated acts which intimidate, offend, isolate, pester, belittle, degrade or humiliate a person or a group of people. He was aware that such acts caused increased absenteeism, turnover, costs, accidents and stress; and at the same time, they reduced productivity, motivation, morale, and customer service.

Julech reckoned that people can find a solution to both the simple acts and the more darker side of unkindness.

He thought, "Maybe what we need to remember is that we are all made in the image of God and therefore there is good in all of us. If people focused their attention on simple acts of kindness that emanate from a sense of goodness, then the more darker side of unkindness will disappear."

Julech had recalled talking to a biologist who told him that even the simplest acts of kindness triggered several chemical reactions. Those reactions helped people reduce stress, become relaxed and happier and relieve low levels of depression.

The bottom line for Julech was that kindness made one feel good and when one felt good it rubbed off onto others.

"Holy smokes it's time to move on!".

He called Chippy, who was high up on the rocks, to join him for a drink of water before hitting the trail. Once they were satisfied, down went Julech's arm, and up went Chippy. They were off until their next break at noon.

*   *   *

The trail was still narrow, and the shale slabs continued to border the trail. Julech kept his eyes peeled on the shale and every once and a while he would stoop to take a closer look. He did want to find some small fossil specimens that he could put in his pack and bring back to Catrela. A couple of small plant imprints or aqua crustaceans would be nice.

Chippy wasn't interested in fossils. He was more interested in taking a nap, after all he spent a good half-hour running up and down the shale looking for grub.

"Funny about Chipmunks, they are always looking for something to eat. They're like the squirrels in our back yard looking for food to keep for winter."

Catrela's favourite squirrel, Big Red, stored peanuts all over the yard. His nest though was up in the neighbor's fir tree. Catrela doubted whether Big Red had horded his nuts in his nest as she kept digging them up every time she weeded her flower beds.

Chippy stashed his winter supply underground in his nest. Julech knew that chipmunks hibernated during the winter. They would go into a deep sleep where their heart beat dropped to 4 beats per minute. Their body temperature also fell while they were in hibernation and equaled the temperature in their hole. During hibernation they fed on their stash of food.

Some of Chippy's squirrel cousins hibernated as well, but they didn't necessarily go into a deep sleep. Big Red, for instance, had a routine of sleeping when it was too cold to go out. When the temperature warmed up, or perhaps when he was hungry or needed to do a bit of business, he landed on Julech and Catrela's patio. He stood on his hind legs and knocked on the patio door for some peanuts then disappeared back to his nest for another sleep.

As he was considering the sleeping habits of chipmunks and squirrels Julech noticed that the trail began to decline and that he had progressed further into a wooded area. The slate slabs receded, and the path widened. He didn't see any fossils on this part of the journey, but he remained hopeful that eventually he would find one or two.

*　　*　　*

Before breaking for lunch, Julech had a couple of more ideas about kindness in the workplace.

One would expect that with all the positive qualities of kindness, people would just naturally act with kindness. In fairness, Julech felt most people did.

"Can we do better?" Julech asked out loud.

He answered his own question in the following way.

"Basically, it's up to each person to act kindly, to take ownership for their own behaviour, no matter what position they have within an organization. It's simply showing consideration for others in such a way that we offer a helping hand whenever needed; or, whenever we see something out of place. We just act to make it right.

Once we get it right with ourselves, we can begin spreading kindness to others. When people see others express acts of kindness they often add kindness to their own behaviour. A simple act of kindness becomes a springboard for others to act in the same way."

Julech thought of Jane again. Being around Jane caused others to take note of her kindness – at least it did for Julech. Why was that?

He thought that maybe it had to do with the act making us feel good, appreciated, and yes, loved. And, it didn't take much to pass on the act. It was all about the golden rule of treating others as one wanted to be treated. A bit of kindness soon transformed into big bundles of kindness. At its core, kindness was all about showing appreciation for the other and in turn feeling good about it.

"What do you think about that, Chippy."

Chippy wasn't listening, he was still fast asleep.

Julech questioned his own acts of kindness. Was his genuine? Did it come from the right place? He felt that his acts of kindness, although small, made him feel good and he did get feedback that others appreciated what he had done.

He kept coming back to the questions: Did he express his kindness in a humble way or was he just soothing his ego? Was he really compassionate in his approach? Or was it a mere reflection of what he felt he needed to do out of politeness, political correctness or just plain courtesy?

Julech remembered what he had concluded when he thought about the compassionate acts of others and said to himself, "Maybe when it comes to kindness, just as with compassion, I shouldn't consider how others act, but be more concerned about how I act. I should work on how to become more compassionate in my approach to kindness."

His stomach began to rumble. The mental work brought on by his musing about kindness and the physical activity of climbing up the trail caused pangs of hunger.

He saw an opening in the path, surrounded by low lying shrubs. A good place to stop for lunch.

*   *   *

The lunch spot had allowed Julech to view the trail as it meandered downward towards the valley behind the peaks of the Three Sisters. At the junction where Fernie Ridge and the Three Sisters joined there was a small pool of water.

He calculated that it could take about three hours to reach that location.

'You know buddy, that's where we'll camp for the night."

Chippy wasn't listening. He had a few acorns left in the pack and was scrounging around to find them. He found one and chipped to Julech to pour some water for him. He then ran around hoping to find a few insects, or better yet, another oak tree. Insects he found, but no oak tree. After his little escapade of running up and down shale slabs and trees he returned to Julech.

"Let's go! Maybe there's more grub at the next stop."

Julech broke off a piece of his energy bar and gave it to Chippy. He popped it into his mouth, stomped up Julech's arm and quickly climbed to the top of the Hat. There he saw where Julech was heading, the pool of water below.

The afternoon hike was a lot easier than the last several kilometres. The trail had wound itself in large U-turns. The further they descended the taller the fir trees and the thicker the underbrush became.

Julech gave his mind a rest and just enjoyed the sights and sounds of the coming forest. He listened as birds sang their mating songs. Every once and awhile one of Chippy's cousins would run across the trail or jump from one tree to the next. When this happened, Chippy would let out a blast in chipmunk-ese, which sounded like "Hi there!" or "Get out of the way we're coming through".

Half-way down their descent to the lake Julech realized that Chippy was awfully quiet. He put his hand to his head and Chippy wasn't there. Nor was he on his shoulder. Chippy was in the pack. There wasn't a chip out of him.

Julech thought that was strange as the sun was beating down and the temperature was about 25 degrees Celsius. Chippy never went into the pack when it was that hot. That was the clue for Julech to look around. Was there danger lurking on the ground or in the trees?

He hadn't seen anything at first, but then off to his right high up in a tree, with one leg hanging down was a Canada lynx.

Canada lynx were meat eaters and they mainly consumed snowshoe hares. However, when food was scarce they dined on other small animals including squirrels. Chippy was no squirrel, but he wasn't taking any chances. He wanted to lay low and be quiet.

Julech hadn't noticed snowshoe hares on the trail. He hadn't seen any lynx either. Lynx were territorial and Julech surmised they were in this lynx's territory. He also knew that lynx were nocturnal hunters and often stashed left-over hare for another day. One snowshoe hare was enough to feed a lynx for two days. Either this lynx was full of last night's meal or it was too hot to hunt, and it was waiting for nightfall.

Snowshoe hares were also nocturnal animals and maybe Julech hadn't seen any because they were sleeping, or it was just too darn hot for them to hop around. Both lynx and snowshoe hares were carnivores, but the lynx pounced on small live animals, whereas the snowshoe hare cleaned up on dead ones.

Julech gingerly walked passed the Canada lynx and hoped that was the last time he saw it for Chippy's sake. He continued to keep a cautious eye on the sides of the trail. Lynx were cats and cats are silent trackers, so Julech wanted to make sure that they were not followed.

A few kilometres later Julech tapped the side of the pack giving Chippy a signal that it was safe to come out. He poked his head out from under the flap, sniffed the air and twisted his head in a 180-degree turn. He was cautiously optimistic that the danger had passed and slowly crawled out to Julech's shoulder and onto the Hat.

The two approached the pool of water which now looked like a small lake.

"I wonder if there are any fish in it, Chippy?"

In typical Chipmunkese came the reply, "I hope not."

The lake was crystal clear and was fed by an equally clear creek that wound its way down from the Three Sisters. It didn't appear that there was an outlet flowing from the lake; Julech guessed that it had a deep basin or crater with tunnels extending beneath the water. At some point down the valley it might surface as a spring or jut out of a fisher and form a waterfall. Julech wasn't sure about his hypothesis but it did seem plausible.

Julech eyed the lake again. Fish would go well with his meal.

After and hour of swishing his line at several spots along the rocky shore he got his answer. The lake was either fish-less or the fish just weren't hungry.

Julech found a patch of sandy beach and pitched his tent overlooking the lake. He found some old wood, dry leaves and small sticks and lit a fire.

He went to the edge of the lake, took off his hiking boots and tested the water. It was darn cold. Nevertheless, he plunged into it like those adventurous people on New Year's Day who took polar dips into the ocean on the northern coastal shorelines.

Chippy watched him with a quizzical look on his face. Julech whistled to him to come join him.

"Are you out of your mind? I'll stay close to the fire."

It wasn't long before Julech was out of the water, dressed and ready to prepare their meal. He had found a handful of editable mushrooms on the way down from the mountain and added them to rice and mixed vegetables. He mixed a package of dried beef soup in a pot of water and added a couple of crackers to thicken it.

Chippy didn't mind the mixed vegetables and rice, although, just like his oats, he preferred them dry rather than cooked.

After their meal they explored the beach around the lake. They had found several different animal footprints. Bears, deer, lynx, rabbits and wolves had visited the waters. The wolf and lynx tracks were disconcerting. Chippy might be vulnerable.

"I'll keep you close to me tonight," he said to Chippy.

"That's a good idea."

Back at the site, Julech stoked the fire to make a cup of hot chocolate, laid back and watched the sun recede behind the mountain. Darkness soon followed and although it was mid July the evening was cool. He wrapped himself in his bag. Chippy had already retired to his cozy corner and didn't seem to worry about wolves or a lynx. Julech put the pack with Chippy close to him.

*   *   *

Julech reviewed his day. His musings convinced him that a compassionate heart led to genuine kindness; that there were plenty of opportunities to express kindness in the workplace; and that individuals had to take ownership for kindly acts.

He postulated that kindness could become a brand for an organization. His experience affirmed that a positive organizational culture began with positive values promoted and nurtured by the owners and the leaders of the business. He thought that if leaders promoted kindness as a purposeful act it would become a genuine dynamic that would bring people together in a positive way, improve customer service, and in the end, provide real financial returns.

Did this suggest that a culture of kindness required more than one or two kind individuals? Certainly, anyone could be kind but surely the culture must be cultivated and strengthened through the personal actions of a leadership team. In time both leaders and employees would experience kindness as a core value and it would permeate the organization

As Julech closed his eyes for the night he committed to grow in the attribute of kindness and to expand his approach to compassion and kindness to include everything that existed. He would explore that the next day.

And so, ended the seventh day.

Kindness Toward Everything

JULECH AND CHIPPY HAD A NOISY NIGHT. FIRST THERE WAS THE terrifying growl of the lynx. The Canada lynx's sound wasn't like the cat's soft meow Julech was familiar with back home. It was the sick cry of a very large domesticated cat. Then it wheezed like the wind whistling through the fir trees. Finally, it gave off cough-like barks.

Julech wasn't sure what had gone on in the bush, but he certainly didn't like the sounds coming from that direction. He didn't know whether the lynx was on patrol for a snowshoe hare or warding off another lynx encroaching on his territory. What he did know was that it had kept him awake and alert.

An hour after the lynx racket had died down and he had settled back to sleep, he was again rudely awakened. This time with the howling of wolves somewhere in the valley south of them. Julech knew wolves roamed in packs and that they could travel long distances in a short time. He also knew that wolves rarely attacked people, but he wanted to be prepared in case they came close.

He got up from his bag, gathered several throwing-rocks, found a couple of large sticks to bang together, pulled out his noise maker from his pack and added a couple of logs onto the smouldering fire. He kept alert and would wait until he had felt assured that the wolves weren't coming his way.

Time passed, and the wolf wails receded. It sounded like they had drifted further south. He relaxed and looked in the pack for Chippy. He was there fast asleep. Neither the lynx growls nor the wolf howls woke him. He had felt safe sleeping in the pack next to Julech.

Day light had broken open too soon for Julech. He wanted another forty winks. Chippy had other ideas. The noisy night hadn't affected him. It was time to greet the day and he chipped as much.

"Go back to sleep!" Whispered Julech.

Chippy wasn't sure he wanted more sleep. After all it was time for Julech to rise and meditate. That's what he had done every morning between 5:30 and 6 AM. That morning was no different.

A constant "get up" chattering came from Chippy, until Julech finally said, "All right, you win. I'll get up."

Julech dressed and splashed cold water on his face. He was ready to meet the day.

Chippy hopped back into the pack and chipped, "I'm alright with God." He pushed his snooze button for another forty winks.

"What a tease you are Chippy," Julech said with a smile.

* * *

Julech asked himself, "What do I mean by spreading compassionate kindness to everything?"

Over the last several days he had found a friend in Chippy, met Clancy's friend Woolly, encountered a variety of birds, watched several deer graze by the lake, caught fish, ate porcupine, came across a bear and a lynx, and heard wolves in the distance. He had been over whelmed with the beauty of the morning and evening skies, the thunder and lightening of a mountain storm, crystal clear lakes, deep valleys, open meadows, rapidly flowing streams and the glorious mountains. All sang a hosanna to his God, and all was a gift of love to him and human kind.

"All of this, and I have just witnessed a tiny slice of the beauty, mystery and majesty of what exists. And, that beauty, mystery and majesty run inward to the tiniest of molecules and outward to an ever-expanding universe." Julech said to himself.

He was again overtaken with the magnitude of it all and once again it affirmed for him that God really did reveal Himself through his creation, if we but listen and look deeply.

Yesterday he had concentrated on how kindness had affected his relations with others. Today he wanted to focus on how he could combine kindness with the natural environment. He felt a further uncovering of that link related to what he had experienced so far.

To begin his meditation he returned to the creation story found in the first chapter of Genesis. There he noticed that the story teller outlined the first two eons (two days in the story) of creation as a preparation for things to come. And what was to come, God saw as "good". This meant for Julech that everything that evolved from those times must be good and worthy of our respect.

He chanted, *Maranatha*

*   *   *

After his meditation Julech went straight to the task of making a hearty breakfast of scrambled eggs, cheese and strong coffee.

Chippy had hop-skipped to the underbrush to see what he could find. Julech was drinking his second cup of coffee when he realized Chippy hadn't returned. He whistled for him, but he still didn't come.

"Did he run into a lynx?"

He whistled again and still no answer. He gripped his coffee cup and took off for the underbrush. He had walked only a short distance when he noticed Chippy clutching and eating a juicy red wild strawberry.

Julech thought that this had to be the place where Clancy found the strawberries he had shared with them the other night. He went back to his pack, retrieved a couple of plastic bags and returned. He picked two bags of strawberries for a later treat.

"That should be enough for us for the next couple of days."

Chippy had his fill of strawberries and chipped, "Ok, lets get onto the trail."

Julech spent a bit of time repacking the backpack, doused the camp fire coals, and stretched out his arm for Chippy to climb to the Hat.

They left the campsite and headed for the trail which hugged the eastern side of the Three Sisters.

The Three Sisters with its angular three peaks was an awesome sight. They were a part of the Washburn Region of the Canadian Rockies, as were all the mountains saddling the trail. The middle Sister was the highest mountain visible from Fernie and reached a height of 2788m.

Geologists had determined the Three Sisters consisted of sloping beds of the enormous Palliser Formation that pushed the 180 million-year-old rock to their height, and like the Fernie Ridge, had been submerged under an ancient sea. The summit of the Three Sisters was comprised of marine limestone formed by the sea bed.

The mountain was officially named the Three Sisters in 1959. Before that time it had two names, the Three Sisters and Mount Trinity. Julech liked the name Mount Trinity because it gave the impression of a three-in-one mountain whereas Three Sisters implied three distinct mountains. Be that as it may, he accepted the name Three Sisters.

"Maybe, I might come across some fossils on this leg of the journey," he said to Chippy.

"Huh?" Chippy replied.

The trail had narrowed and became rugged. It followed a rushing stream that flowed into the lake where Julech and Chippy camped for the night.

*　　*　　*

As he walked up the trail, Julech's mind turned to the beauty that surrounded him and again thought about how his culture took "Mother Earth" for granted, and how humans were slowly choking the life out of her.

"We wouldn't do that if we truly appreciated her as a gift for all of us to behold, protect, nurture and respect. We are living in extremely perilous times." He chanted sorrowfully, we live in...

A time when we have the power to destroy all that exists on earth through nuclear warfare.

A time when we see whole species of animals vanish.

A time when we experience tremendous destruction caused by climate change.

A time when greed seems to overtake generosity, temperance and reasonableness.

A time when people try to take the place of God and forget they only exist because of God.

A time when great transitions give rise to fear, anxiety and worry.

He thought if we fully understood that all matter – people, animals and inanimate objects found in our universe – was connected and infused with the Great Spirit then we would have a different approach to our world and everything in it.

He conjectured that over the centuries the western world had separated matter from the Spirit. Ancient wisdom people hadn't done that, nor did many of the great philosophers and theologians. They saw a deep connection between matter and the incarnate God as the indwelling of the Spirit in all things.

He surmised that when people began to separate matter from the Spirit they were strengthened in their belief that it was ok to destroy the gift we had received.

He said to Chippy, "Perhaps when we lost the notion that the Spirit existed within animals we lost respect and kindness toward them. And when we didn't accept that the Spirit existed within the land, we raped and pillaged it for selfish gain; and when we failed to see the Spirit within others, we sought to conquer them through conflict, violence and war."

He then cried out, "All of creation is a gift. Can't we graciously accept that?"

He noted that when someone had received a gift the person usually cherished it, thanked them for it, and often gave it a place of honor.

He again cried out, "What happened to us who have received the greatest gift – all that exists? Where is our thanksgiving, our sense of cherishing and our respect and kindness it deserves?"

Julech didn't want to sound too simplistic, but maybe that was the answer. Humans in their quest to conquer the known and unknowable had complicated the simple. They had fractured the unity of all things and lost the 'goodness' of God found in them. They created a new tower of Babel.

"Maybe to appreciate and show kindness toward the natural world we need to return to a deeper sense of simplicity – to a sense of the holiness in everything." Julech softly said to Chippy.

Chippy bent down from his perch and squinted into Julech's eyes and said in his most formal chipmunkese voice,

"You see that's why I'm alright with God. You humans are consciously destroying the land in which we all live; and now you are sending stuff into the atmosphere. For what? To conquer that too?

Me and my fellow creatures, live in harmony with the land, and only take enough to fill our needs, and no more. Our harvest is about keeping a balance within nature. There is enough of everything to go around.

Those that are predators are predators only to feed themselves and their families. We don't hoard stuff like you humans. Nor do we kill or maim out of greed or wipe out whole species. We have fights but there are no wars among us. Our fights are usually about protecting our selves or our families, or, he paused, you know over a mate during the mating season.

Sure, I need to hide once and awhile because of a goshawk or a lynx but I understand that and so do they. That doesn't mean we don't see the 'good' in each other. We respect each other for our own good and the good of the other.

The other day when you threw rocks at the porcupine you wanted to scare it away. When you accidently killed it, you didn't hold it up as a trophy. You carefully prepared it for a meal. And, last night when you took some precautions because you feared the wolves and lynx, you wanted to scare them and protect me as well. In all those actions your approach was kind and respectful and your intentions were honorable.

Finally, our natural world lives in the now. It doesn't worry about tomorrow. Tomorrow will take care of itself. We don't worry.

Yes, we live the simple life. You should try it."

"Thank you, Chippy," Julech said sheepishly.

*　　*　　*

Julech had been hiking up a steep incline. The stream to his right was now rushing down like a waterfall. He looked ahead and noticed a trail veering off to the left and heading up the side of the Three Sisters. It was narrow, rocky and clung to the edge of the mountain. He had come to a fork in the trail. The last stanza of *Robert Frost's Poem, The Road Not taken* came to his mind.

Julech was ready for a challenge and he said to Chippy, "Let's take the route less traveled."

"Oh brother. I'll be safe, but I don't know about you."

About half way up to the summit, a mountain goat had joined them. It had jumped off a small ledge onto the trail and acted like a guide. It nimbly tipped toed ahead with ease. Julech wasn't so graceful. He slowly and cautiously struggled up the incline.

The Three Sisters were home to mountain goats. Julech often looked at the goats on the cliffs through a set of binoculars. He thought they were a strange breed.

Mountain goats are members of the antelope family. They sport scraggly beards, strong muscular forequarters and pliable hooves with soft under pads which help them gain traction on rock surfaces and keep safe under harsh conditions. They are agile and like to scale high places where they can rest under a canopy of overhanging cliffs. They are active both day and night and move around the mountains according to the seasons.

Male goats are loners or hang out with two or three male buddies. However, they are known to fight their male counterparts over a female during mating season. Female goats are called nannies and usually spend several months in herds looking after their kids. They too can be aggressive especially when they detect that their kids are in danger.

"Did humans call their nannies and kids after goats or was it the other way around?" He asked Chippy.

"How do I know? By the way, what are nannies?"

The goat that was ahead of Julech was a male loner and didn't mind leading the two hikers up the trail. Julech wasn't sure where the goat was headed but he was happy to follow it.

The trail had tapered to a narrow goat path. Mr. Goat was fine, but Julech had started to worry. He looked down on his left side and was faced with a sheer drop. If he fell there was no telling what might happen. The path grew steeper.

He reached into his bag, lifted Chippy to his shoulder, removed the *Chapeau* and put on a helmet. He didn't want loose rock bouncing off his head. Just as he was considering turning around and backtracking the goat jumped off the trail and hopped-skipped up to limestone buttress, laid down and looked at Julech and Chippy.

"Does this mean were at the end of the trail?"

Chippy who was still at his post on top of the hard hat observed the trail ahead. Yes, the trail was tapering off. No, this wasn't the end of it. He had seen what Julech couldn't see. A bank of snow and ice further up the trail.

"Keep going."

Somehow, Julech understood this bit of chipmunkese and kept moving. Vigilantly.

It wasn't long before Julech saw what Chippy observed and where Mr. Goat was leading them. A glacier. It wasn't big, but glaciers didn't have to be big. It wasn't like the ones found in the Canadian Arctic Archipelago, but it had all the markings of a glacier. A thick layer of ice on the bottom and hard crusted snow on top. It had to be the glacier Clancy talked about the other day.

The trail led up to the top of the packed snow where Julech could easily step onto the glacier. He did so gingerly and looked down into the valley below. He could see where the water trickled off the ice and formed small creeks. They joined the stream beside the path the two hiked on the way up and ended at the mouth of the lake where they had camped the previous night. It was a stunning view.

Chippy jumped from his shoulder when he removed his pack.

Julech had felt a bit woozy from the height and tried to forcefully breath in oxygen and exhale carbon dioxide. Pressure breathing didn't relieve his dizziness, so he took an altitude sickness pill.

The snow shone with a bright sheen. It was crunchy and sparkled like a chandelier. It was also solid. Julech was able to stand on it without sinking.

This was all new to Chippy. Snow and ice clusters weren't something with which he had experience. He sat on the snow, patted and tasted it and understood that it was cold. After he was satisfied that it was something he could deal with he jumped up and down, almost dance-like, ran around and tried to toboggan on his back.

Julech picked up grasshoppers, flies, beetles and spiders from the snow. He cupped them in his hands to warm them and they began to hop and fly away. The winds had lifted the insects up to the glacier and because of the cold they went into a state of suspended animation. The warmth of Julech's hands woke them up and freed them from their deep slumber.

As soon as Chippy saw the insects fluttering about he had a field day trying to catch them. Then he began to look for them in the snow. He wanted to taste frozen insects for lunch.

"Not bad." Chippy crunched one frozen treat after an other.

Julech watched in amusement. He gazed again at the sights below. From this height he began to put more things into perspective.

*　　*　　*

He had come to the realization that he had an affinity with animals. He came to that conclusion earlier during his hike, but now he felt he had a clearer understanding of what that meant. Yes, it had to do with coming from the same Source, but that understanding was more of an intellectual exercise, now he felt it more in his heart. Chippy helped him with that new insight when he had chipped away at him about the animals that he had met along the way.

When he thought about the sad laments he had earlier he began to realize that there were at least three approaches we (he used 'we' as a way to include himself) could take to turn things around.

> First, we can continue to search for opportunities to control the destructive damage we are causing the environment – and much of that rests with each individual as well as a collective effort. Individuals should be able to find something they could do to reduce the negative impact on Mother Earth. Collectively, and in collaborative and cooperative fashion, governments at all levels should continue to promote and expand policies aimed at protecting our natural resources – after all they are in our best interest and our children's children best interest.

> Secondly, we can learn to live simpler lives. This doesn't mean going back to the stone age, but it does mean becoming aware of the waste we create and doing something about it. It also means downsizing our wants, not our needs, and stop listening to the advertising mantras of large corporations to purchase more just for the sake of having more.

> And thirdly, and this is huge, we need to shift to life sustaining spiritual values. We have to keep

reminding ourselves that everything is connected, and we have a sacred mission to protect, preserve and nurture the whole.

Julech got up and looked for an exit from the glacier. He didn't want to leave this rarefied air, but he knew he had to get off the glacier and find a place to camp before nightfall. He looked back to the trail that led up to the glacier. If he took that route he had to backtrack and that would cause a three-hour delay. Not that a three-hour delay mattered but if there was another trail on the other side of the glacier that would be his preference.

He walked across the glacier to investigate. There was another goat path heading downward to what looked like a clearing. The path appeared treacherous, and easy for goats to travel – for Julech and Chippy, maybe not so easy.

Julech looked at Chippy. Chippy stared right back at him and chipped, "I'm willing, if you are."

"That's easy for you to chip, but I have to do the downclimbing."

"Aw, go ahead. I'll be with you. You can do it."

On came the pack, up went Chippy to his shoulder, on went the helmet, and down they went to the goat path.

Julech carefully walked the path. There were deep crevasses on one side and high smooth rock walls on the other. Parts of the wall were wet and slimy from water trickling down from the glacier. He was an experienced hiker, but he didn't like being a goat. If there was another way he would have gladly taken it.

He cautiously pushed his feet downward using the bottom of his boots as friction against the loose stones on the path. The stones were slippery and covered with moss. He was extra cautious.

It wasn't a fast descent to the next level where the path widened, but he eventually got there. He let out a deep breath and looked back up the path. There was Mr. Goat on a high overhanging slab of limestone looking down. He nodded his approval, turned and jumped away.

Chippy tapped Julech's hard hat and chipped, "See I told you, you can do it." He then dropped to Julech's shoulders and crawled into the pack. He had been confident in Julech's ability to reach the widening trail, but he wanted to keep vigilant watch just in case he had to jump to safety. Now he was ready for a nap.

*　　*　　*

On the descent, Julech thought about how he could identify with the so-called inanimate objects, like the rocks, sand, dirt, and water. He wanted to tie in his previous conclusion which suggested that everything was connected and made whole in the Spirit.

"I understand now how I have a kinship with animals and all living things but how do I relate to 'real' matter," he wondered.

He once read that Indigenous people had such a close connection to the earth that they enjoyed walking with bare feet or with moccasins. That way they could feel a closeness to Mother Earth and hear her "heart beat". They had an emotional connection to the earth that was hard for Julech to fully appreciate.

Then he thought of Catrela and how she had often said, "I can't wait to get my hands in the dirt". Had she been referring to the enjoyment she had in planting her garden? Or, was she actually enjoying the feel, smell and closeness to the ground like a spiritual awakening? He thought he knew the answer to those questions but now he wasn't so sure. He hadn't really asked her. He would have to do that when he returned home.

"Maybe if I take a different approach it will come clearer to me how I can relate to 'real' matter," he pondered.

It wasn't immediately apparent to him, but he gradually considered his own body as a starting point. Ninety-nine percent of the mass of his body was made up of water, carbon, nitrogen, calcium and phosphorus; and, chemicals such as sulfur, sodium, iron, magnesium plus a trace of other elements. The only metal it didn't have was aluminum, the third common element on the earth's crust. And that was because aluminum was harmful to humans.

"I'm a walking chemical and metal container," he sighed.

He came back to the opening story of Genesis and remembered how God fashioned humans from dust. (Genesis 2:7) He doubted whether the story teller knew the link between the common chemicals and metals found in dust and in humans.

He remembered that the story teller also said that God breathed upon the human to give it life. He breathed in His Spirit and gave humans what some call their 'soul'. Therefore, he reasoned, he was materially connected to the earth and spiritually connected to his God through the creative act.

Julech again went back to his thoughts about the unifying source of all that exists and existed.

"Aha!' I'm related to inanimate matter because I'm composed of the same stuff."

He stopped and picked up some pebbles and dirt and let them run through his fingers. He went over and drew his hands through the long grass bordering the side of the trail. He put the palms of his hands onto the trees. And, for a few moments he began to feel an empathetic response to both animate and inanimate matter.

"I wonder if my friends will regard me as a *tree hugger*?" He let that sink in for a moment and then said to himself, "Kindness to matter, matters."

*   *   *

After a couple of hours downclimbing on the wider tail the two reached the meadow that he had viewed from the glacier. He had to take extra care for the first half of the path as it was tricky, risky and narrow. However, he was able to make good time on the last half. Julech was thankful that he had took the 'route less traveled' and that he hadn't had an accident on that trail.

The meadow was filled with field flowers, birds and insects, especially mosquitoes. It was the first time on his journey that he had to pull out the bottle of mosquito repellant to ward off the bloodsucking pests.

Julech found a spot near a creek to camp for the night. The water from the creek was cold, clear and refreshing. He remembered that the headwaters of the creek were from the glacier but wasn't sure the creeks tributary waters were safe to drink. He filled his canister with water and as a precaution, he popped a purifier tab into it. He then pitched his tent with a built-in mosquito mesh. He didn't want to be bothered by those pesky things during the night.

He built a smudge to keep the mosquitoes at bay for the evening and built a second fire for cooking and warmth. For the last several days Julech found that he needed to put on his jacket during the evenings. He was enamored with the sunsets, but after the sun had set the evenings had cooled considerably. He missed the warmth of the day's sun.

After the smudge was lit and the mosquitoes abated, Chippy poked his head out of the pack. He had enough sleep and it was time to explore his new surroundings.

The meadow was fenced with pine and fir trees and underbrush. A few trees along the edge of the stream further away from the camp caught Chippy's eye. So, he headed in that direction.

Julech had a full day of hiking and wasn't in the mood for any exploring. On the descent he noticed his knees were getting sore and wobbly. 'Elvis knees' experienced hikers called them. He just wanted to eat and crash for the night. He would wait for the morning to do his exploring.

For the first time since he began his hike he didn't feel like cooking. He pulled out his peanut butter concoction, a couple of dried left-over biscuits, dried fruit and some pieces of beef jerky. He made a large cup of soup and looked into the fire to review his day.

*　　*　　*

He had started off his day lamenting about how people harmed themselves by harming nature's bounty. As he hiked that day he realized he could have a kinship with all living things as well as with the mountains, streams, rivers and even the unfolding cosmos itself – he could show kindness to all that existed.

Despite the self-evident warning signs that "Mother Earth" had been sending to humankind, he felt that he could look to the future with hope. He was upset with the climate deniers but felt there was a growing awareness about the impact of wanton destruction of the earth's atmosphere. He was pleased to learn about how people were being attracted to a simpler life style. And, he was heartened with the mounting evidence that everything was connected and, in his mind, holy.

He lamented the extinction of species, the destruction of forests and the streams, pollution of rivers, lakes and oceans, and the catastrophic and disruptive weather patterns caused by damage to the atmosphere. He wanted to believe that all of these signs of an earth in trouble could be abated. For Julech, hope by itself was not a strategy and so he wanted to promote continued action to mitigate the damage to "Mother Earth".

In addition he wondered whether nature's own healing process could be an antidote to some of his world's ills.

He recognized that his body had the uncanny ability to heal itself. When he cut himself, developed blisters or bruises he realized it healed itself. Sometimes though the lacerations needed ointment or tape to help the healing process. Other times his body was seriously sick and required medical attention. That's when he went to see a doctor. After added medication or an operation to cut out infection or repair damage his body had healed itself and became stronger or whole again.

Like his body the earth also had the ability to heal itself. It could replenish its lakes and streams with fresh water. It had a natural renewal process where nature's rhythm slept, awakened, shot forth new growth, slowed down and slept again. Natural fires destroyed deadwood and allowed forests to regenerate, and, animals lived in harmony and established a mutual life balance.

Julech knew that the earth now required help. It could regenerate its streams, water, forests and atmosphere but we needed to help it by stopping our destructive ways. If we did that, rivers would flow clear, forests would come back, and the air we breathe would be clean again.

"But he said, it's just not up to others to fix I too must do my part to contribute to the healing process."

Once again, he recalled what the first hiker he met said, "Open your eyes and ears. Look and listen deeper." Julech now realized that to look and listen deeper he needed to do so with his heart, his mind and with compassionate kindness to everything.

*　　*　　*

Chippy's timing was impeccable. He had returned to camp just as Julech finished his review of the day and was about to snuggle into his bag.

Julech wasn't sure where his little friend had gone. It didn't matter. For it was time for him to call it a day.

Chippy crawled into the pack and Julech looked up to the heavens and ended his day with a song of hope:

> It's a time when the findings of science support true religion.
>
> It's a time when there is greater awareness of the harm we are doing to our earth.
>
> It's a time when there is re-birthing of endangered species, forests and water.
>
> It's a time for returning to the wisdom of the ancients.
>
> It's a time for spiritual renewal.
>
> It's a time for greater openness toward others.
>
> It's a time for kindness toward every animate and inanimate thing.

And so, ended the Eighth day.

Three Peaks of Humility, Forgiveness and Joy

CHIPPY CRAWLED OUT OF HIS CORNER, HOPPED ONTO JULECH'S chest and patted his face. He heard a friendly chip, "Get up!"

Chippy's pat was reminiscent of Catrela's cat. Her cat had patted her face every morning to wake her up. It was her gentle alarm clock. Julech wondered if all small animals had the same habit once they formed a friendship with humans. He would have to investigate that later. Now it was time to check out what was happening outside.

He unzipped the tent and stuck his nose out. It wasn't cool. It was darn cold. He looked to the sky. It was overcast with dark clouds. Not nice.

"It's so cold I can see my breath!"

"Is it going to snow?" asked the Chip.

'I certainly hope not."

Last night the temperature had been muggy, and the air had been filled with torpedoing mosquitoes. Now, there wasn't a mosquito in sight. Because of the unsettled weather, he questioned whether he should press onward or stay put for the day. He would make that decision after his meditation and breakfast.

Chippy had usually crawled back into the pack while Julech was meditating. He didn't do that. He jumped out of the pack and tent and went straight for the bush. Julech thought that was strange but didn't consider it any further.

The temperature had a damp coldness about it which chilled Julech to the bone. He put his jacket on, flipped the built-in hood over his head, and tossed his sleeping bag around his shoulders. All bundled up he looked like a homeless man sitting beside a store front on a cold winter's day.

Perhaps, he had felt the cold because it was such a contrast to the hot days he had experienced so far on his journey. No matter, he was warming up and ready for his morning meditation.

*   *   *

He ended last night on a hopeful note and wanted to continue in that vein. However, there was one more thing he needed to consider in his relationship with the outside world. The experiential 'aha' moment he had yesterday was a significant breakthrough. For a time, he felt a deep kinship with nature. He wanted to continue exploring that relationship.

He knew his tendency was to relate to things objectively. He noticed that he had referred to certain animals as an 'it'. They were more objects than subjects. Some animals such as the porcupine, goshawk and lynx were an 'it' and others he had given names, like Blacky the bear, Mr. Goat and of course Chippy. He wondered if he had called an animal which seemed more distant to him an 'it' and those who had seemed friendlier a personal name. It seemed the more friendly and familiar animals became the more he saw them as subjects rather than objects.

Julech realized that this might be why Francis of Assisi named objects, like the sun and moon, Brother and Sister and had such a close connection with animals and all of nature. He had personified everything as subjects and not objects. He related to them intimately recognizing the holiness within each as the creative indwelling of his God.

It occurred to Julech that he might relate to people as objects. He was proud about his knowledge concerning interpersonal relationships, after all, he had spent most of his life working with people by helping them improve the way they treated others.

Maybe that's the clue, 'he prided himself on his knowledge'. He was knowledgeable about relationships, but had he treated others as 'objects' rather than 'subjects'? He hoped not.

To help people work through their issues, he felt he had to steel himself from their feelings and any feelings he had about them. He had to be objective and not get caught up in his or their emotions. In this self-protective stance, had he really understood what people were feeling? Or had he just dealt with the technical aspects of the relationship?

When he had worked with his clients, he identified their feelings and emotions. He had them express and name what they were feeling. Was he objectifying the exchange or was he fully engaging with them in a compassionate and empathetic way? More importantly did he objectify the relationships he had with those close to him?

Julech sensed that even in his most intimate relationships, whether they were with family or friends, he tended to objectify – he was always in 'work' mode, solving problems and seeking answers rather than listening and accepting.

Catrela had often said to him, "get real Julech," and "you need to become more empathetic". Did she mean that for him to be "real" and "empathetic" he needed to dig deeper within himself in order to express greater human intimacy? He added those questions to the growing list he wanted to explore with Catrela.

Julech realized that he had to peal away more of his ego and the armour he used to protect his true self. It was high time he put away his pride and become 'real' to himself and others.

"Be completely humble and gentle; be patient, bearing with one another in love." (Ephesians 4:2)

He chanted *Maranatha*, give me strength Lord to be humble.

*   *   *

Chippy returned and stared at Julech. His eyes were bright and dancing. He had found something, and he wanted to share it with Julech. He was like Julech's favorite puppy Sam, wagging his tail with its tongue hanging out. He ran part way to the bush and returned and did the same thing over again.

Julech finally got the hint.

"OK, I get it. Let's go take a look."

Chippy skipped in front of Julech. "Look!" he chipped and ran up to a bunch of saskatoon berry trees. Julech could tell he was pleased with his find and so was Julech.

The saskatoon berry was known as the serviceberry, prairie berry, shadbush, and juneberry. It was a wild plant native to Western Canada and usually found from the Great Plains to the coast of British Columbia. The name originated from a Cree word which meant 'the fruit of the tree of many branches'. The berries had made excellent jams, pies, crisps and wines. All of which Julech enjoyed.

How the trees had landed in these parts Julech didn't know. He knew that at one point the saskatoon berry was known as pigeon berry. Was it because pigeons liked the berries? Or, was it because they carried them from place to place, dropped them and they took root? He wasn't sure about the answer to those questions. He settled on his own theory. They were brought here by humans or by animal poop.

The trees were about three and half meters high and filled with ripe berries. Enough to feed an army. He looked around to see if there were bear tracks or droppings. He found none.

"How lucky can we get?" he said out loud.

Chippy chipped, "Very lucky."

Julech went back to their little camp and picked up a couple of bags. Saskatoon berry 'something' was going to be on the menu that day.

He returned to camp, gathered several old dry logs and lit a brisk fire. He made a large pot of porridge and supplemented it with berries. He wanted to make a pie but instead baked an open-fire saskatoon crisp. That would be dessert for later in the day.

After breakfast Julech looked to the sky. It still didn't look kindly and the temperature remained cold and damp. However, it didn't feel like it would rain or snow. Chippy seemed to agree with that assessment.

Julech liked camping at the base of the Three Sisters. He felt a sense of comfort there. So, rather than pushing ahead on the Black Gold trail he decided to use his campsite as a staging point for taking a side hike. He had heard that there were caves in that area. He wanted to search for them.

Julech took a hard look at Chippy. It appeared he had put on weight in the short time they had hooked up together. Perhaps he had spent too much time sitting and navigating on Julech's head and shoulders.

" When we go hiking today, my little friend, you're going to do more walking,"

"Who me?"

Julech poured water over the hot coals and made sure it was completely out. He packed up his tent, bag and cooking gear and headed over to where Chippy had found the saskatoon berry trees.

Earlier, when he was picking berries he had noticed a trail heading toward the opposite mountain. It seemed to gradually meander up to the treeline. It didn't look like the hazardous trail he had hiked yesterday that had led up to and down from the glacier. This trail appeared to be an easy climb.

"Maybe it will bring us to a cave," he said to Chippy.

"Ya, maybe." Chippy replied as he strolled beside Julech. He preferred to be on top of the Hat then down on the trail. He was chipping an awful lot. Probably grumbling in chipmunkese because he wanted to ride rather than walk.

*   *   *

As Julech leisurely hiked the trail, he had noticed a lack of chatter, bird songs, and other noises coming from the forest surrounding him. Perhaps the heavy overcast and dampness kept the animals bedded down.

Outside of the crunching of his boots on the trail, the odd chip from Chippy, and a soft whistle from time to time caused by a slight breeze through the trees, there was silence. It was going to be a peaceful walk up to the tree line.

Julech absorbed the gentleness of the swishing trees and the quiet noises coming from his boots scratching the ground. He was in the space between the words, a contemplative state where he was taken up with the beauty of natural setting but oblivious to it. He was experiencing solitude but not loneliness. Runners and hikers had called it, "in the zone". He was glad he had Chippy with him. He would alert him to any dangers along the trail.

Julech was experiencing a sense of peace and inner joy. A joy that was hard to explain.

He felt content, happy and joyful, like the 'happy wanderer' whistling away as he hiked along his trail. He knew that sense of happiness or joyfulness would quickly disappear if he encountered a grizzly bear. It would turn into fear. He also knew if something untoward happened to Chippy his happy-joy would turn into sadness.

The inner joy that Julech was experiencing was different. It wasn't a "happy pill" type of joy. It had come from his relationship with his God. It grew out of a spiritual connection born out of love.

It was almost like what Chippy said in the mornings, "I'm alright with God." Julech sensed that he had said "I'm alright with God" because he understood God's deep love and that his little life was a song of praise to Him.

Julech's feeling of joy was something akin to that. He was experiencing a quiet confidence that said to him no matter what happens everything will be alright. His God will always be at his side in love. Julech's feeling of joy had welled up within him as he released himself to this great Love, and in return he received an inner joy that he couldn't fully comprehend.

He gradually recognized that it was a gift of grace bestowed upon him from another facet of Love's great diamond.

"Could a sense of joy last through some of the darkest times in life?" He asked himself.

Slowly the answer came to him as he reflected on someone he had known.

Noella always had this sense of joy. In her teen years she had a serious accident, which left her with a crippling disability. She suffered dearly with pain and at least once a year was admitted to the hospital for painful treatments. That went on for several years until eventually her body succumbed, broken and withered .

He had known Noella as a living saint. No matter how she felt, she always greeted visitors with open arms, a smile and a joyful demeanour. She had a confident trust in God, lived for the moment and knew no matter what happened to her body she would be alright. Noella had shared her gift of joy with others despite her pain and suffering.

*   *   *

Julech looked at his watch and estimated he had a couple of more hours left before he had to return to base camp. The trail took him up the side of Mount Bisaro. Julech had read that the largest cave in Canada and perhaps North America was located on Mount Bisaro. He wanted to find that cave.

"Let's get going," he said to Chippy.

This time Chippy wasn't going to walk ahead, beside or behind Julech. He needed to navigate. Before Julech could bend down his arm to let Chippy climb to his *Chapeau*, Chippy had crawled up Julech's leg and backside, climbed onto his shoulders and jumped onto his perch. Chippy was ready to look out for anything that might impede the hike.

In the quiet of the hike he took in the sights and sounds.

Suddenly Chippy was thumping on Julech's head. He wasn't chipping as he usually did. He was just thumping.

Julech took that as a warning sign. Had Chippy seen something that wasn't in Julech's sight? He stopped.

Chippy kept on thumping.

Julech didn't see or say anything. He just listened and moved his eyes from side to side.

He heard it.

A grunting sound came from the bush ahead.

Julech wasn't sure but it sounded like a grizzly bear. Did he have a premonition earlier when he was musing about joy and fear – a fear of a grizzly bear? Julech was about to find out.

He squinted and searched the trees and bush. He didn't see anything. He heard more grunting.

Julech had learned about the behavior of grizzly bears from his friend, Andrew.

Andrew was a woodsman and had spent many years wandering the mountains and backwoods surrounding Fernie. Whenever there were grizzlies in the area, Andrew went out to watch them. He came to know their sounds and behaviour. Andrew had gained notoriety for his knowledge about grizzly behavior. He was often called upon to lecture and run workshops on the grizzlies for those hiking in the woods.

Julech listened carefully to the grunts. A grunt could mean a signal of friendliness or a command from a female to her cubs.

Grizzlies could be aggressive toward people, but generally tended to avoid contact with them. It was important for Julech to find out if this bear was a female, because females were known to become aggressive if they perceived that their cubs were in danger. All the female had wanted to do was protect her offspring. Whether it was a male or a female, grizzlies always let others know their intentions. They did this through their body odor, language or sounds.

Since Julech couldn't see the bear, it was critical he listened to the sounds. So far, he only had heard grunts. He listened for teeth clacking, huffing, popping jaws, snorting, screaming and bawling. *Teeth clacking* could mean the bear felt threatened or there was something in the vicinity that he didn't like. It was a signal to "back off." *Huffing and snorting* could mean it was agitated, fearful or aggressive. *Popping jaws* could mean the male was engaging in aggressive behaviour or a female was alerting her cubs.

He continued to hear only grunts, so he still wasn't sure whether it was male or female. He continued to listen.

He knew that male grizzlies rarely *bellowed* which was a talltale sign of aggression particularly when they competed for females in the mating season. He knew that female grizzlies would also bellow especially when they needed to defend their cubs.

Julech heard none of those sounds. Yet!

He was well aware that he he should never aggravate grizzlies. They were bigger, stronger and more powerful than him.

Grizzlies could weigh up to 700 kilograms and stand 3 meters tall on their hind legs. He had seen grizzly claws. They were long and sharp. He also had viewed pictures of people who had been viciously mauled by grizzlies. They weren't pretty.

He knew that grizzlies liked all kinds of fruits, insects, honey, nuts and all sorts of fish and animals, including those like Chippy. And they had great noses. They could smell a small pack of food a mile away. He hoped the grizzly wasn't hungry as he had a supply of goodies in his pack.

Julech quietly pulled out bear repellant and the bear horn from his pack. Andrew had taught him that bears would retreat 90% of the time upon being sprayed with bear repellant. It would also back away from an air horn blast.

The bear grunted.

Julech blasted his air horn.

The bear stopped grunting.

Julech stopped blasting.

Silence.

Julech held his breath.

He heard another grunt. This time further away.

Julech blasted again.

Silence.

No grunting.

No sound and fortunately no aggressive noises.

After all that cat and mouse activity, Julech still wasn't sure he had heard a grizzly. He didn't care. The grunts were gone, and it had moved on.

From that point on every time he turned a corner he sang out loud or blasted the air horn.

Julech and Chippy had hiked above the treeline and were near the top of Mount Bisaro. They had come across impressions in the ground called 'choked sink holes' and happened upon a small cave. He wasn't impressed. It wasn't the famous Bisaro Cave.

It was noon, the weather had warmed, and the sun had broken through the clouds, but the temperature was still chilly.

Julech said to Chippy, "it doesn't feel like the middle of July."

Chippy responded in a chipmunkese laugh, "I don't mind, I have a fur coat."

Julech sat down to give his legs a rest and have a bite to eat. He scrounged around in the pack and found the wild strawberries, beef jerky, peanut butter and honey balls, nuts and a package of dried mixed vegetables. It didn't look like much, but it was a meal Chippy would like. He laid it out and they both munched together as they overlooked the valley.

Julech had decided not to trace the same path back to base camp. His compass sense said that if he kept above the treeline and cut across the mountainside he would eventually join the trail that had brought them to the top of mount Bisaro.

That route was a relatively easy walk.

*　　*　　*

Julech returned to his mornings meditation and his need for greater humility, and his thoughts turned to forgiveness.

He understood that forgiveness was about releasing anger or resentment toward someone or someone's behaviour. It also included excusing somebody's mistake, wrongdoing or misunderstanding. He felt the sentiment, "I forgive you," had tremendous meaning both for the giver and receiver.

He said under his breath, "It's easy to say, 'I forgive you' or 'I'm sorry' but to apologize and ask for forgiveness from the heart may not be so easy. That often takes humility, vulnerability and courage."

Julech knew there were times when he had lost his temper and argued with others. Sometimes those disagreements were significant and other times they were not. It was easy for him to say, "I'm sorry," when he was apologizing for something that wasn't difficult but when he knew he had offended someone more deeply – well that was harder. There were times he didn't know how to approach the person on those more difficult occasions.

In some ways he had felt humiliated and vulnerable when he sought forgiveness. He felt humiliated because the very act of asking for forgiveness showed him that he wasn't perfect after all. He felt vulnerable because the other person might see him as weak. In both instances they pointed to his sense of self-importance and pride.

He also found it hard to ask for forgiveness when he believed he hadn't done anything or said anything wrong. In those situations, he often became defensive, brushed off his comments as trivial and at times resented the individuals for even thinking he had offended them.

However, he didn't feel he had resented others for any length of time. He knew that there were times when he became self-defensive, held on to his anger, and gave people he loved the silent treatment or was sarcastic toward them. When he caught himself in that state he tried to rectify it as honestly as he could and then asked for forgiveness. He thought those acts, important as they were for seeking forgiveness, were nothing compared to what some people had experienced.

He remembered Jake whose son had been shot and killed in the school yard, not too far from where Julech lived. John could have been angry for the rest of his life. He could have been filled with resentment or overcome with revenge. Instead he went to the young boy who shot his son and forgave him.

John told a small crowd of people who had gathered around him after his son's funeral, "It wasn't an easy thing to do, but I had to do it otherwise my anger and resentment would destroy me."

Another person, Michael, had been wrongfully committed to prison for murder and kept there for almost fifty years. When he was finally exonerated he said he had "forgiven" those who wrongfully found him guilty and held "no grudge" toward them.

Then there were those who had forgiven each other during the "Truth and Reconciliation" process in South Africa and during the reconciliation process between the First Nation's people and those within the broader Canadian community.

"Those stories of forgiveness and reconciliation should be an inspiration for us. It must take great courage to confront and truly forgive those who had deeply hurt them," he said to Chippy.

Chippy didn't hear him, but Julech figured he would have agreed.

Julech realized that it was easy for people to say, "I'm sorry" and "I forgive you." He felt it would be harder for them to free themselves from the resentment or anger and removing those feelings could take some time. However, if they didn't do it they could be consumed by them. On one side holding back forgiveness, and on the other side keeping anger and resentment bottled up within could cause great emotional pain and affect relationships with others.

This led Julech to believe that the first thing people needed to consider was to forgive themselves, because it is the self, who holds the resentment, anger and grudge. It was a reciprocal process binding both forgiveness and forgiving. And once the healing was experienced through forgiveness and forgiving they could go on with their lives.

He thought of Gloria again and how she overcame her resentfulness and learned to love again.

Julech felt that the examples of the acts of forgiving that he had just thought about were empowering acts. They had reduced people's burden and expressed their strength of character and the character of those involved. He had observed that when people engaged in reciprocal acts of forgiveness, mutual trust, openness, understanding and compassion grew.

"Yes, the road to reconciliation isn't always easy, Chippy, but it is necessary for both individuals and communities if they wish to reach closure and a respectful outcome."

"Good point, Julech."

*　　*　　*

As Julech turned the next corner, there it was, the Bisaro Cave. And what a cave it was. It was massive. The mouth of the cave was enormous. It was almost the size of Julech's house. He never saw anything like it in his entire life.

Julech learned that the cave was at least 670 meters deep and 5.3 kilometres in length. Explorers started mapping the cave in 2012 and named it *Bisaro Anima*. It was the deepest cave known in Canada and geologists say it might be one of the deepest in North America. Explorers had yet to reach its bottom. Throughout the exploration they had encountered cold temperatures, complete darkness, waterfalls, crawl ways, irregular floors, loose rock, constricted pathways and a large pool of water.

Julech was not about to explore the inner sanctum of the cave but when he walked into it his eyes grew as big as watermelons. He was completely amazed.

Julech and Chippy went a few meters into the cave, sat down beside a trickling water fall and took in the damp, musty smells. The light from the opening had filtered through to where they were sitting and bounced off the walls, ceiling and water. It was a magical sight.

Julech imagined early tribesmen in the cave. He didn't see any drawings on the walls or anything that had indicated early dwellers. That hadn't stopped him from fantasizing about indigenous people finding shelter in the Bisaro after a hunt or a small clan making it their home. In his mind's eye he imagined venison or moose meat roasting on an open fire.

Julech wanted to stay in the cave longer, but he had to get back to base camp. As he walked out of the darkness he was met with a brilliant light that dazzled him. He was overcome with emotions he couldn't explain. It was like moving from the shadows of life with an indwelling of an unknowing flickering flame of love to being embraced by the brightness and radiance of the fullness of life fueled by a blazing fire of Love. He stood in the heat of that glow for what seemed to be an hour but in real time was only a few minutes.

That experience shook him but once he recovered he looked forward to traversing Mount Bisaro for a few more kilometres. The path joined the trail he had taken earlier that morning and it wasn't long before he was back at base camp at the junction of Fernie Ridge and the Three Sisters.

The first thing Julech did when he returned to camp was to search for a log or felled tree. He remembered the grunts of the grizzly and he needed to build a bear post. He found something better, an old dried out white-washed tree trunk with branches sticking out about three and a half meters high.

"Perfect." He looked around to show Chippy, but he wasn't around.

He set up camp about 5 meters away from the bear post.

In the meantime, Chippy had remembered the previous evening's excursion and scampered over to the saskatoon berry trees. He was hungry from all the navigation he did that day and couldn't wait for Julech to lay out a meal for him. He needed something to eat.

It was still cool, but not as cold as it was that morning. The weather had tempered the mosquitos so there wasn't a need for a smudge. He built a fire to warm up soup, macaroni and cheese, coffee and the saskatoon crisp he had made earlier that morning. He set out a peanut butter ball and two pecan nuts for Chippy.

He whistled for Chippy to come and eat. Chippy came prancing back but he was in no mind for food. He was filled with Saskatoon berries.

Julech ate and sat back to nurse another piece of saskatoon crisp with his coffee. Chippy joined him. He had room for a bit of crisp and a sip of coffee.

"We had a superb day, didn't we Chippy?"

"Yup! I didn't like the sounds of the grizzly though."

Julech had seen things that he would store in his memory bank for life particularly his potential encounter with a grizzly and the awesome Bisaro Anima Cave. He was glad he climbed Mount Bisaro and used the junction between the Ridge and the Three Sisters as a base camp. He was thankful it hadn't rained, and for the coolness which kept the mosquitoes at bay.

Before he bedded down for the night, he put the backpack with all the food, utensils and hygiene material up high on the bear pole. As a final precaution he hung up his smelly clothes on the pole too. Chippy would have to find a corner in the tent to sleep and forget the pack for the night.

Julech rolled up in his bag, looked up at the three peaks and gave the Sisters new names. He called one Humility, the other Joy and the third one Forgiveness. An old name given to a new born female child was Humility, meaning "meekness before God". A more common name for a female was Joy which originally meant "joyful in the Lord"; and Maghfira was an Arabic female name which translates as Forgiveness with a meaning of "standing in awe of God".

And so, ended the Ninth day.

The Conversation – Love Serves

IT WAS MORNING. JULECH OPENED ONE EYE AND PEEKED OUT OF the tent. He looked over to the bear pole. Grizzlies hadn't visited during the night. That was a good thing. The air smelled crisp and clean. He looked to the sky. It was clear. He was warm in his bag and wasn't ready to crawl out of it. He checked for Chippy. He was curled up in the corner still fast asleep.

Julech had been in a semi-sleep when he heard voices. First a male than a female. They were talking and giggling. He opened the tent flap and saw them pointing to the bear pole. His clothes were on the pole. Julech was in the tent. He was almost butt naked. He wasn't amused.

George and Jen had camped further up stream and wanted an early start. They had been hiking for about an hour before they stumbled upon Julech's campsite.

"Hey, can you please hand me my clothes?" shouted Julech.

"Well I don't know, maybe you should come and get them," George replied.

Jen laughed.

"Aw come on, I said please."

Chippy chipped with a grin on his face, "Go get them Julech, I dare you."

Chippy moved to the furthest corner, where he could see the bear pole. He wasn't going to miss this opportunity for anything. He wanted to see Julech prancing for his clothes while the three of them watched.

Jen came to Julech's rescue.

"Grab his clothes, George. Don't embarrass the guy."

Now George was a short fellow and try as he might he couldn't reach them.

Julech watched.

Chippy waited in anticipation. "Maybe this is going to play out as I hoped," He chipped gleefully.

After a few more jumps at the clothes, Jen again came to the rescue.

"Bend down and I will climb up onto your shoulders."

He did, and she did. She pulled on the clothes. They came lose and she fell back off George's shoulders. She came down with a thud.

"Are you alright?" yelled Julech.

"Yes, my dignity hurts a little though."

George took the clothes over to Julech.

Chippy curled himself into a small ball. George didn't see him. Chippy was happy about that. He befriended Julech, but these people were strangers.

Julech slipped on his clothes, exited the tent and greeted his visitors.

"Hi, I'm Julech."

"Hi, I'm George and this is my partner Jen."

Julech learned that George and Jen were a couple from Calgary. They owned a business that employed 75 people. They said they were stressed out and wanted to get away for awhile. They often came to Fernie to ski, but never to hike. They decided that hiking would be a good release for them. Their hike had started at the north end of the trail and they were to end up at the Lodge where Julech had started his hike. There, another couple were to meet them.

Julech explained that he was on a journey of self-discovery and that he too had just finished a stressful project and needed a break. He told them about the discoveries he had made along the way with special attention to the Bisaro Cave and the glacier up the side of the Three Sisters.

Once the introductions were out of the way. Julech asked them if they would like to join him for breakfast. "We already have had breakfast, but wouldn't mind a cup of coffee." George and Jen said in unison.

"Of course," Julech said, "as long as you don't mind me munching away on my cereal."

That wasn't a problem for them.

"Besides skiing and hiking, what else do you do to reduce stress?" asked Julech.

Both chimed in that they had a gym membership and tried to run regularly.

"How's that worked out?"

"To be honest, it hasn't," Jen responded.

"How come?"

"We're just too busy and can't find the time."

"What do you mean, by that?"

"Well as soon as we get up we check our emails and telephone messages and that dictates our day," George offered.

"We feel we have to answer those emails and telephone calls immediately or else things would pile up. Soon we're inundated with more emails and follow-up calls. Then we're off to the office and more stuff comes at us," Jen added

Julech summarized, "Let me see if I got this right. You gave up your trip to the gym and your run, and each time you did that you had fewer workouts and runs. Days go by and you realized you hadn't worked out for a week or weeks."

"You got it right," said George.

"Then you came to a point when you felt burnt out and needed an extended break. Am I still right?" asked Julech.

"Yes," replied Jen.

"Who is taking care of your emails and telephone calls now?"

"Well, we appointed someone to review them as they come in and answer the urgent ones. For those that required our input, we asked her to set them aside and forward them to us when we had access to WI-FI."

"So, you had delegated the responsibility to someone you trust and who could filter out the important from the urgent while you were away. Is that what you did?"

They both answered in the affirmative.

"Why can't you do that on a regular basis?" Julech asked.

The two looked at each other but didn't say anything.

"It seems to me you had made a decision that workouts were important to you. They were necessary to avoid burn out. When you actively pursued physical activity on a regular basis, you felt better, had more energy and got more accomplished. Right?"

"You got it!"

"And you found ways to delegate responsibility and certain levels of authority while you are on this hike. Right?"

"Right!"

"When you get back to your business, why don't you continue the same pattern. That way you can attend to one of your high priorities about looking after yourself. I think in that way you will be able to deal with others more effectively. What do you think?"

It was if a light bulb went on. George said, "Well damn, that makes perfect sense."

"Here are a few more pointers that may help you, George. One of the last things you should do before you leave the office is clear out important unanswered emails, review unattended tasks you weren't able to accomplish that day and carry the important ones over to the next day. Of the tasks you carry over determine which ones you could delegate. Finally identify three priorities you wish to accomplish the next day and complete at least one of them before you read your morning emails. These are tried and true techniques which will help you get ahead of the game. If you faithfully follow them you will learn to manage your day, rather than your day managing you."

Jen pulled out her phone and dictated a message to herself relating to Julech's suggestion.

She then pulled George aside, "We have lots of time to finish our hike. Let's ask Julech if he has the time to spend the day with us and explore some of our other leadership issues."

George thought about it for a few minutes and agreed.

Julech considered their request. He felt that even with this unexpected day out he could still meet Catrela on the agreed-to day and place.

That's how it all began – a conversation with Jen and George about serving with love as leaders.

*   *   *

It was nine o'clock and normally Chippy would be sitting on the *Chapeau* exploring the trail with Julech. Here he was, still in the tent. He checked outside and saw the three people in deep conversation.

"What is this?" He chipped to himself. He needed to do his morning constitution, and he hadn't had breakfast or his morning coffee. He was beside himself, stood up in front of the tent flap and began yelling in chipmunkese.

The three couldn't help but hear the ruckus.

"What's that rodent doing by your tent?" Jen asked Julech.

Julech explained that Chippy was no ordinary rodent. He was his companion who travelled with him for the past eight days. He told them how he came to befriend Chippy and some of the experiences they encountered.

Chippy watched the three of them with piercing eyes. He wasn't sure if he could trust the newcomers. He crawled on his stomach to the end of the tent and then made a bee line to the edge of the bush. He would have a saskatoon berry breakfast and maybe find a few insects to top it off. He would miss his coffee though. Maybe those two guys would leave soon and he and Julech could get on with it.

*　　*　　*

Jen opened the conversation with her observation about how they dealt with their employees. She said they drove themselves and their employees so hard that they often questioned whether it was worth the effort. Their company was doing well. Every year they made more profit than the previous one and their customer base had grown year over year.

"Our business is prospering because we are in the driver's seat. We push, push and push. Our employees don't seem to appreciate how hard we work. It seems all they want to do is wait until the buzzer goes off at five o' clock and then make a fast exit out of the office," Jen said.

They liked their paycheque though," George countered.

"Do your employees get along? Do they work effectively together as a team?" Julech asked.

"Generally, they do get along," Jen offered, "but there is a lot of bitching among them. Sometimes the bitching is directed at us and other times they direct their anger at each other. I have often told them, 'grow up or find another job.'"

"One other question, how high is your turn over rate?"

"Funny you should ask that question. We used to have a high turn over rate but since last year it has settled down," George said.

"Maybe that's because we're experiencing a downturn in the economy," Jen suggested.

"Maybe," George said, quietly.

"Do you love your employees?" Julech asked.

"Love?" George looked over his glasses, "Love?"

"We pay them well for their work. We make sure they have extra health and wellness coverage. We don't expect them to work on week-ends and if they do they get paid overtime. I'd say we care for them in that way, but 'love'. I don't know. Do we love our employees Jen?"

Jen looked at George and then at Julech. She didn't know what to say.

Finally, she said, "Love is a strong word. It relates to deep feelings for someone. I love George and he loves me. We're intimate with each other. Are you asking if we are intimate with our employees?"

"Heaven's no!" exclaimed Julech. "You are referring to love as something sexual. That's not what I mean. Can you imagine love as something other than sexual?"

"Well I love our dog Ginger, but I'm not intimate with her," George offered.

"I hope not!" Jen laughed.

"What do you mean when you say you love your dog, George?"

"I have feelings for Ginger. I care for her. I have positive feelings for her. In a way I guess I love our employees too because I care about them."

"What happens when your employees make mistakes or cause disruptions in the workplace? Do you still have positive feelings for them? Do you still love or care for them?"

"I get angry. I can't say I still 'feel' the love for them," George said.

"What happens when your dog does something you don't like? Do you still love her?"

"Of course," said George, "she is an animal and I can overlook her shortcomings."

"So, if your employees do something wrong your feelings of caring which you equated with love, disappear. You get mad. But, if Ginger does something wrong, you still care or love her. Let me ask you this: do parents still love their children when they do something wrong?"

Jen and George shifted on the log where they were sitting. "Of course, they do," they said in unison.

Julech asked the two if they knew what '*philia*,' '*storge*' and '*agape*' meant.

"Never heard of them," each replied.

"They are Greek words for three different kinds of love.

> *Philia* love is the love people have for others when they consider them to be close friends. It's a friendship love. Close friends often share the same values, interests or activities and get along with each other. Sometimes we hear someone say, 'I love that guy'. They don't mean it in a sexual way, they mean it as a close friend.

> *Storge* love relates to affection that exists within a family. It is the affectionate bond between a parent and child or between brothers and sisters. It can be described as a natural love arising out of an unexpected relationship.

Agape love means unconditional 'love.' Early Christians used it in a variety of ways. For instance they used it to describe God's love for us; Christ's love for all, and the love they had for each other. It's a love that says, 'no matter what happens, I will continue to love you'. Christians view agape love as the highest form of love."

George looked at Jen and said to Julech, "You forgot one other kind of love. The love Jen called intimate earlier."

"You're right George, the Greeks called that *Eros*, where we get the word erotic from. That's the passionate love between two people which often results in the birth of children."

"So Julech, what kind of love were you alluding to when you asked, 'do you love your employees?'" Jen quizzed.

Julech turned the question back to her.

"What do you think?"

George took a stab at the question. "Well, its either a *philia* love because we're trying to bring everyone together with the same purpose and values; or its an *agape* love. Maybe *agape* love would be hard to realize in the workplace."

"I agree," said Jen.

"Maybe it's not either-or. Maybe it's both. For now, let's consider love as both *philia* and *agape* and just call it 'love' and see where that takes us."

"Fair enough," Jen and George said.

Julech detected some hesitation in their voice and suggested they take a break and do a little leg stretching.

The three hikers kept their conversation going as they strolled across the meadow.

"Earlier we talked about the stress we were under and you said we needed to take care of ourselves so that we can care for others. Perhaps you meant, we need to love ourselves so that we can love others,'" Jen suggested.

"That's the way I see it," said Julech, "without getting religious, Jesus said 'Love your neighbor as yourself.' I suggest one interpretation of this is that he was getting at this type of love. A love where we take care of ourselves, not in a selfish way, but in a way that we have the energy to look after others. Maybe a way to look at it is for us to become selfish so that we can be selfless."

"I like that," Jen said.

"What else do we need to know about love?" George queried.

"The love we're talking about can be summed up in a simple phrase, 'love acts'. It's about how we act toward one another. It's not about feelings, it's about the decisions we make or the choices we make to do something. Those choices have a bearing on how we behave toward others."

"Can you give us some examples," Jen asked.

"First, let me ask you a couple of questions," Julech replied.

"When you love or care for someone or something what do you do? Or if someone loves you, what do you expect?"

"Well I hope I would be kind, generous, authentic, and honest," George said as he looked at Jen.

"I would add patience, respect, gratitude and resilience," Jen offered.

"And, I would suggest forgiveness and humility to your list," Julech said.

"You see," said Julech, "these are all behaviours. Kindness, generosity, authenticity, honesty, patience, forgiveness, gratitude, respect, humility and resilience are ways of behaving. And all of them flow from the word love."

"I never thought of it that way," George said.

Jen agreed.

George looked confused.

"Are you perplexed about how all this applies to leadership?"

"You read my mind," George responded.

"What does leadership mean to you, George?"

"It's about directing people. Telling them what to do and getting things done. I'm not a coddler. We have a business to run and we have money to make. If people don't do what I expect them to do, they're gone. I want my employees to run things by me. I make the final decisions on everything down to the last detail. In many ways I'm like Attila the Hun, it's my way or the highway."

"You got that right," Jen said. "Everything is measured against the bottom line. We push our employees to the finish line. We do get a lot accomplished that way."

"Sounds like there might be a lot of fear among your staff."

"Fear is good, I want them to be afraid. If they don't perform they know they are gone. Period!" George said with a determined look.

"You also said, you have a high turn over rate and you get stressed out from overwork. What is that telling you?"

"Your comments earlier gave me pause about they way I delegate. That's one thing. I'm not sure how we deal with the turn over rate though," George said.

Jen looked at George and quietly suggested, "Maybe we have to do things differently, George."

The way in which Jen said, "maybe we have to do things differently George", suggested to Julech that Jen may also be afraid of George.

"Let's look at leadership from a completely different perspective and examine how it could apply to your business," Julech proposed.

"Shoot," said Jen. George looked sceptical but was open to hearing more.

"Let's turn your leadership concept upside down George. Rather than leaders acting like dictators where they perform as if they are masters of everything, I'm going to suggest that they are servants who support and develop their employees. After all, if leaders of businesses didn't have employees they wouldn't be able to lead. I'll base this type of leadership on 'love' and the behaviours of love. Remember, love acts."

"Oh brother, this should be good," George said under his breath.

Julech suggested they consider *kindness,* one of the words George used to describe how he would act with someone he loved. He flipped back to his notes he made about kindness earlier during his journey and shared them with his new friends. He indicated that his findings revealed that leaders who champion kindness in the workplace have reaped significant benefits from their employees and from their outreach within their community. Kindness improved their bottom line, engaged employees in a purpose beyond the dollar, and made everyone feel that they were contributing to something bigger than just going to work to earn a pay cheque.

"We are kind to our employees," said Jen.

"Are you, kind? Or are you just abiding by the labour laws and regulations?"

"We feel the work they do is worth more than the minimum wage, so we pay them more," George offered.

"It seems to me you are paying them for what you think they are worth. That's more about justice than kindness. Kindness would be about showing employees appreciation outside of their pay cheque, listening to their concerns without passing judgment, promoting a project like *Habitat for Humanity* and giving them a few hours off to contribute to building houses, or having appreciation days for employees. Do you get my drift?"

"Yes," said Jen. "We can do some of those things George. It wouldn't cost us very much and it could go a long way toward improving our work environment."

George responded with, "Let me think about it."

Julech suggested that they approach kindness from an investment perspective rather than a cost perspective. He then turned to a word Jen used to describe how she would act with someone she loved. *Patience.*

"Now that is an area where we fall short, Jen," George offered.

"Let's talk about how you dealt with situations where patience was required."

"We get back to push, push, push," Jen said. "We just keep things moving. We have little time for talk, talk, talk. At times we get down right angry especially when employees make mistakes. We have no time for that. We say, 'get with the program, or else.'"

"It seems to me when we're dealing with employees and customers, patience is a pretty big deal," Julech offered. "Patience is about accepting and tolerating delay without getting mad or upset. When people get angry and upset they spew venom to everyone in their way."

"Yes, we do a lot of screaming and yelling. Got to keep things moving, you know."

Julech asked, "Do your employees really listen to you when your yelling and screaming?"

"Sometimes I wonder," Jen said.

"I asked about fear a little earlier, and you said it was important. It seems to me your lack of patience causes fear and may destroy any chance for innovation or new ideas to come from your employees."

"How so?" asked George.

"For instance, if one of your employees, let's say Susan, makes mistakes and she is always chastised for them, do you think she will try something new on her own?"

"She can, but she has to come through me first," George said.

Jen countered, "But George, you're so busy you don't have time for them. You don't even listen to them. I'm a bit that way too. Why would our employees come to us, if we always shut them down? Why would they try something new? They would be afraid of making a mistake and get blasted for it."

'Hmm, I see your point, Jen, however, they need to be held accountable."

"You're right," Julech said. "You should hold them accountable if they make a mistake, but you can take a different approach. You can still hold them accountable while maintaining their dignity. You see, making a mistake is healthy. Often that is how we learn and how innovation takes place. You can use the mistake as a learning opportunity rather than using it to dress down someone. Here's an example:

> There is a story that occurred in the *Old Shoe Factory* where an employee tried a different way of making shoes. It didn't work, and several thousands of dollars were wasted. The boss asked the employee to come and see him. The employee was sure he was going to get fired. Instead, the boss asked him what he learned from the experience. The employee listed several things he would do differently if given the chance. The boss said to him, 'Well you have your chance. I want you to build on what you have learned, and my suspicion is we will have developed a better shoe.' The employee was surprised and said, 'I expected you to fire me for making such a big mistake.' His boss looked him in the eye and said, 'Fire you. Why should I do that? I just invested thousands of dollars in your education.' The next year a new shoe hit the market which turned out to be one of the best sellers for the Old Shoe Factory."

George and Jen got the message. Patience and allowing mistakes go hand in hand.

"One more thing. Patience also tones down the rhetoric and makes for a more peaceful workplace," Julech added.

George looked at Jen, "Boy I sure will have to bite my tongue. Our employees won't know what happened to us, if we developed this approach."

Julech was getting hungry and he suggested that they break for lunch.

"We covered a lot of ground this morning. Perhaps we should let that settle over lunch. We can tackle a few more topics after we eat."

They both agreed.

*   *   *

"They're not gone yet?" Chippy chipped.

Julech noticed Chippy and motioned him to come over for some lunch. He put out some nuts and peanut butter balls for him.

Chippy looked at the nuts, stared at Jen and George, and slowly stepped over to the little pile that Julech laid out. He lifted the nuts to his mouth and kept his eyes on Jen.

"He's a cute little fellow," Jen said.

"Cute, I'll have you know I'm the best-looking chipmunk in these parts," he said in chipmunkese fashion.

Jen and George didn't understand him, but Julech did and he smiled at Chippy.

After lunch Jen and George took a walk around the meadow. That was fine with Chippy. He crawled over to Julech, climbed on his shoulders and up to his perch on the Hat. He would watch those two to make sure they weren't up to something.

Julech for his part, realized he hadn't meditated that morning. He was convinced that great leaders are those who put service first. He hoped Jen and George would take heed about some of the things they talked about that morning. He was convinced one can be a strong leader by making choices based on love.

He repeated his mantra. *"Maranatha."*

Now Chippy knew what was going on with Julech and his mantra, but for Jen and George that was another story.

They came back from their walk and saw Julech sitting straight up with his hands on his knees. He appeared calm and peaceful. Chippy sat quietly beside him.

Jen and George kept their distance and just watched. Chippy jumped on Julech's knee and started thumping. Slowly Julech opened his eyes and focused his attention on his surroundings. He saw Jen and George and smiled at them.

"What was that all about Julech?" asked Jen.

Julech told them about his daily practice of mediation and how it helped him connect to his God and in return how he gained insight about compassion, forgiveness and love. He talked about how his monkey mind was tamed, and how it also helped him to relieve his stress. He gave a short history about meditation and highlighted its resurgence in the last thirty years.

He explained how Jen and George could enter meditative states, apply the Japa technique and the three-minute method he used to relieve tension while at his desk.

They listened with keen interest but weren't sure they would take it any further.

Jen wanted to learn more about leading by serving with love. George was still struggling with the concept but was willing to continue.

"What do you want to know more about?" asked Julech.

"On our walk George and I talked about how *generosity, gratitude* and *respect* can be bundled up with kindness, but we were unclear how leaders show *forgiveness* and *humility*. We also had differences of opinion about honesty, authenticity and resilience."

"Let's see if we can tackle a few of these 'love behaviours' in the time we have left. Let's start with *honesty*. What are your differences of opinion?"

"Jen says honesty and authenticity are one and the same. I think they are quite different and I don't think we can be honest all the time."

"What is your view, Jen?" Julech asked.

"I don't think you can be honest without being authentic; and, I don't think you can be authentic without being honest. Basically, honesty is about being truthful and living a moral and ethical life. Authenticity is about being transparent or being true to oneself. If someone is honest she will also have to be authentic."

'You are correct in your interpretations Jen, but aren't you defining the two as well as expressing their differences."

"Maybe I can be authentic and not be honest."

"How so?"

Jen replied, "Well, if I really believe that telling 'white lies' is ok, and I consistently tell white lies, maybe I'm being true to myself. Another way of putting it would be 'what you see, is what you get,' but I'm not really telling the truth, and therefore I'm being dishonest."

Jen glanced at George.

"Does a leader need to be both authentic and honest?" Julech asked.

"Yes!" said Jen.

"No!" said George.

"Why do you say 'no' George?"

"Because there are times when you have to tell white lies."

"Oh?"

"Well, get real. There are times when I can't tell an employee about something, so I fudge it."

"So, you're dishonest with them?"

"Yes."

"And do you do this with other relationships as well?"

George looked at Jen.

Jen said, "Yes."

"Does this have a bearing on your leadership style, George?"

"Well sometimes I get tripped up on it?"

"By who?"

"Well sometimes by Jen...sometimes by our employees...and sometimes by others."

"Will others think less of you, George?"

Jen didn't wait for George's answer, she replied, "Yes."

George answered, "Well, maybe."

"Here's my take on it, George. When we're honest and therefore truthful we build trust with people. When we break trust, it is extremely hard to repair. There is no need to fudge the truth. If we can't divulge something for confidential reasons we can say so, change the subject or better yet, don't say anything at all. Just don't comment on it. It seems to me when we tell so called 'white lies' they are still lies, and we begin to lose credibility. Ultimately people get confused about whether we're telling the truth and begin to question our motives."

"I don't do it that often," George said.

"You do it more often than you think you do," countered Jen.

Julech explained his understanding this way:

"Sometimes it takes courage to tell the truth – to tell it like it is. It's easier to hide behind the fudge. When we exhibit that kind of behaviour we are often trying to be the nice guy. We're wanting to be liked.

In a leadership role we need to be honest with employees about their behaviour, particularly if they are not performing appropriately. We can use poor performance as a learning opportunity for them and help them develop a stronger character and in the end be a better employee. We try to help them reflect on their own behaviour and change it to something more appropriate. It requires a lot of listening, understanding and empathy. And, like we said earlier we do it in a way that maintains their dignity.

I know a leader who has no hesitation in correcting his employees. When he does so, he always says, 'I love you anyway'. And, he says that in a very kind and gentle way."

"I don't know if I can go that far," George said with a slight smile.

Julech also suggested honest and authentic leaders continually strive to build positive relationships, strong organizations, and express their true feelings. They are self-aware and work at keeping their ego's in check; they don't try to impress with show boat antics but with genuine concern and empathy.

Jill summed up the conversation with the comment, "It seems then, that when we act with honesty and authenticity we act with integrity, build trust and develop employees."

"Wow, that's impressive Jill!" George said in amazement.

"It's time to stretch again. Let's go for a stroll." Julech said.

"That's a great idea," George said.

*　　*　　*

The three hikers followed the stream and came across a gentle waterfall with a deep pool at the base. Julech's first inclination was, 'are there fish in there?'; while Jen's was 'gosh it would be nice to take a dip'; and George seemed somewhat detached, he was still rolling the last conversation around in his head.

The water was clear and cold. They filled their water containers and headed back to camp. On the way back, they heard a loud commotion coming from the saskatoon berry patch. Julech immediately understood the chipmunkese yelling. The other voice he couldn't make out.

They went over to investigate. There was Chippy defending his peanuts while a blue jay was squawking at him with great intensity. Blue jays are known to be loud and aggressive. It was puffed up to do battle. It had been feeding on the berries but when it saw Chippy's peanuts, it wanted them. Chippy would have none of that nonsense.

Julech came to Chippy's rescue and chased the bird away. Blue jays were smart birds. That one tucked this little episode away in its birdbrain and said to himself, "I'll be back."

Chippy settled down and followed the three back to the camp. He sat outside the tent and watched Julech, George and Jen.

*　　*　　*

Julech started the conversation with, "You wanted to know more about *forgiveness.*"

"Yes, this seems a strange word to use in the workplace," Jen said.

"Yes, it is," Julech agreed. "It's a word we rarely hear."

Julech summarized his notes about forgiveness.

"Forgiveness is about removing anger and resentment for something someone said or did; or excusing somebody for a mistake, misunderstanding, wrongdoing or inappropriate behaviour. It's more than saying I'm sorry. It's saying I'm sorry and asking for forgiveness or forgiving someone who said I'm sorry and meaning it."

"Well, I do say I'm sorry when I've done something wrong," Jen offered.

"Do people say, I forgive you?" asked Julech

"Not really."

"What about when someone makes a mistake and says I'm sorry. Do you say I forgive you?"

"Not really."

Julech pointed out that asking for forgiveness shows our vulnerability and affirms we're not perfect. In the workplace people make mistakes, because they are not perfect either. Forgiving them releases them from fear and allows them to grow and develop better habits. Forgiving them also releases our own anger and frustration.

"You said this morning that you get angry when people make mistakes. Do you think you are doing yourself a disservice because of that?"

"In a sense, yes, because I'm the one who is angry; and sometimes this boarders on resentment. I take it personally," Jen said, as she lowered her eyes.

"You see, you are holding it in. Maybe you need to forgive yourself and in that forgiving you may be in a better position to forgive others."

Julech again referred to his musings about forgiveness and pointed up to the Three Sisters. "I named that peak, Forgiveness," He said.

While Jen and Julech were talking George was silent. Julech could see that he was trying to absorb what was being said and trying to figure out how to apply the conversation to him. Julech left him alone in his silence.

"What about *humility*?" Jen asked.

"Well," Julech offered, "if we recognize we're not perfect, and accept our vulnerability and practice forgiveness in its truest form, humility comes."

"That's linked to pride," George pipped up. "Pride is important. It shows that we want to be the best and we're achieving great things. I'm proud for what we have accomplished. I don't want to walk around with my head hanging low in humility."

"You don't need to do that George," Julech offered. "It seems to me that there is a place for both pride and humility. Pride is related to self-esteem and belief in one's worth, and a certain amount of pride is important for us and our teams, but pride can be overbearing, boastful and arrogant. When pride gets expressed in those terms it interferes with our relationships. If we spend too much time believing we are the greatest and puffing up our ego, then all the things we talked about that make for a positive work place become diminished."

"Doesn't pride give us confidence?" Jen asked.

"Depends what you mean by that Jen. Confidence is about having a firm conviction in our abilities and that we are all right. We can have confidence without inflating our ego with pride. Humility has less to do with confidence then it has to do with being self-righteous. I know because I feel confident about what I do but I have to watch how I do it. Sometimes I can get pretty self-righteous."

"Ok, I'm getting a better understanding about how humility and leadership go together. Can you give me a couple of ideas about I can project a humbler attitude?" George queried.

"Here are a couple of ideas," Jen said. "Rather then promoting something as if you did it, give credit where credit is due. I think a humble leader would put others first and praise the employee for doing it. Another way may be to let go some of the control you think you have. You have power because other people have given it to you. I read somewhere that if we hang onto power its like hanging on to one candle. One candle in a dark room doesn't shed much light. If we give power to others its like lighting the whole room with a bunch of candles. There's more light and everyone gains. I suggest a humble leader is a candle lighter."

"Gee Jen, where did you get your wisdom all of sudden?"

"I don't know. Maybe I'm beginning to realize that this concept of leading with love makes sense after all."

Julech sat back and watched the couple bounce ideas off each other. He heard a different approach to working with employees than the one he heard earlier that morning.

Julech quietly got up and lit a fire. It was time to celebrate the day. He checked his pack. There was enough mac and cheese for three, dried vegetables that would cook up nicely in boiling water, and flour to make flat bread and saskatoon berries for dessert.

Jen and George were so taken up with their conversation that they were unaware that a cook was busy preparing a meal, that is until Julech clanged a pot and called them over.

"My goodness," said Jen, "I'm sorry we could've helped."

"No problem. You're my guests."

"I've got something to add to the menu."

George went over to his pack and pulled out a wine skin. "I think this will go well with the flat bread. Now we can really celebrate the day."

The image of breaking bread and sipping wine in celebration wasn't lost on Julech.

After they ate, they sat around the camp fire. Julech and George with a cup of coffee and Jen with a cup of hot chocolate.

Jen spoke in a quiet voice, "I'm sure glad you agreed to spend the day with us. I believe I speak for George, when I say we learned a lot today. We will be talking about serving with love for the rest of our hike. It will change our whole approach to how we relate to our employees."

"I agree, and maybe the love we're talking about is really about agape," said George.

"By the way, what do you call the other two peaks?"

"Humility and Joy."

"I understand now why one is Forgiveness and one is Humility, but why Joy?" Asked George.

"Well," said Julech, "If we put into practice what we talked about, we will experience inner peace and joy."

The hikers lifted their packs onto the bear pole. Jen and George set up their tent. Chippy settled in his corner and Julech rolled up in his bag. Before Julech fell asleep he reviewed his day. He said to himself, "If leaders committed to serving with love, people would enjoy going to work."

And so, ended the tenth day.

Returning to Love.

"When I lose myself in the timeless now and not worry about
the little things that disturb me I become free to spend
a moment with my God. And if I can string those moments
together everything I see, hear, touch, smell or do becomes
important as they are driven by the Spirit of Love."
Julech

A Walk Through the Forest

Julech was awakened with loud squawks that had pierced the quiet of the break of day. Chippy jumped up, he knew that sound, and he didn't like it. There, on top of the bear pole was the blue jay, jabbering away in his language at the pack. Bluey knew that there were nuts in there. Julech didn't know how he knew, but he knew.

Chippy would have none of it. He gave his best warning screech in Chipmunkese. The pack held his nuts and there were only a few remaining for the trip home.

Julech said to Chippy, "Hey, we can share. You had your fill along the way."

Chippy looked at him. He understood, but he wasn't happy.

Julech went over to the pack. Bluey flew to the highest branch on the pole and waited. He knew he was going to get what he came for.

Blue jays had a hard time just accepting a few goodies. They would come back time and again for more. For some reason after Julech dropped a couple of peanuts it didn't return. Maybe Bluey was teaching Chippy a lesson or two.

The noise woke up Jen and George. They stumbled out of their tent to greet the morning.

Chippy looked at them, "They're still here?"

"Never mind, Chippy they will be leaving soon," Julech whispered.

"Praised be the Lord!"

"Good morning!"

"Good morning, it looks like we're going to have a beautiful day," Julech said as he eyed the azure sky. There wasn't a cloud in sight and the temperature was already warming.

The three filled themselves with scrambled eggs, left over saskatoon berry crisp and coffee. Chippy, who by this time had become a bit more familiar with the two guests sat close by and munched on dried fruit and a peanut butter ball.

George had been ruminating about yesterday's conversation and said, "There is one more concept we didn't touch upon yesterday. *Resilience.* I view resilience as the capacity to quickly bounce back or have the flexibility to move forward when we face adversity or blocks in our progress. Maybe we need to take detours along the way, but we still have to move ahead without sacrificing our vision or values. I can see I will need a lot of resilience to put the tenants of servant leadership into practice. I know I'm going to have many days when I will slip back to old habits."

"Me too," said Jen, "but if we commit to the process in an open and honest way we can do it. We can support each other as we learn together."

She paused and then turned to Julech.

"We feel we just scratched the surface on serving others with love. We still have a lot to learn. Can we call or email you in the future for help?"

"Absolutely, here is my telephone number, email address and a website you can use as a resource."

"You know, Julech, I was skeptical yesterday. We're non-believers and I felt when we started we were going to get into a lot of 'Jesus stuff'. That didn't happen, and I can see how this new approach could work for us."

'You're right George, anyone whether they are a Christian or not can apply this approach."

Julech considered exploring this further with George but reckoned it wasn't the time nor place. He said under his breath, "God loves you George and Jen and whether you believe or not you will be participating in God's goodness and love."

The three hikers packed up their belongings and headed in different directions. George and Jen were in deep conversation as they crossed the meadow. Chippy was at his station on top of the Hat.

Julech got as far as the end of the meadow and sat down.

"Now what?" chipped Chippy

"I would like to sit here below the Three Sisters one more time before we move on."

Chippy instinctively knew what Julech was up to. He hadn't meditated that morning.

He chipped, "OK, I'm alright with God. You go and meditate, I'm off to the saskatoon berry trees one more time."

Yesterday's conversation with Jen and George led Julech to a quote from St. Paul:

> "Love is patient, love is kind. It does not envy, it
> does not boast, it is not proud. It does not dishonour
> others, it is not self-seeking, it is not easily angered,
> it keeps no record of wrongs. Love does not delight

in evil but rejoices with the truth. It always protects,
always trusts, always hopes, always perseveres."
(I Cor: 13:4-7)

There was a lot of meat in that one quote and echoed the
whole concept of servant leadership.

It occurred to Julech as he meditated on Paul's attributes
of love that they could apply to everyone even if they didn't
act in a formal leadership role. "Each one of us can become
a self-leader in our own right and reflect those attributes in
our relations with others and with everything that exists," he
said under his breath.

He then turned inward and chanted *Maranatha.*

*   *   *

Chippy returned. He jumped on Julech's knee, chipped and
thumped vigorously.

"Ok, Chippy, let's go. You know this is the last leg of our
journey. I can't wait to get back to Catrela. She will meet me at
the Ferris Creek bridge, and unfortunately you and I will have
to part company."

"Oh?" With that, he hopped back on Julech's shoulder and
onto the Hat. He would continue navigating as long as they
were hiking.

"We are going to hike around Mount Proctor, the base of
Mount Hosmer, then follow the trail along the highway and
stop at Ferris Creek" Julech said to Chippy.

"Whatever," was the chipmunkese reply.

Shortly after they had left the meadow there was another
fork in the trail. One went up along the ridges of the mountains
and the other traversed along the valley.

Julech took the valley trail. He felt it would be an easier hike and he would be able to make up the day he lost while talking with Jen and George.

As they turned north-west Julech asked, "Chippy, do you know how the Three Sisters and Mount Proctor got their names?"

"Nope, but I'll bet I'm going to find out."

> "Well according to an ancient legend an Indian Chief was smitten by three young maidens and couldn't make up his mind about which one he should marry. When the Elders asked the gods to help them choose, the gods weren't pleased and punished them for their indecisiveness. They turned the young chief into Mount Proctor. The maidens were so sad that they asked the gods to turn them into a mountain too – and from that time on the mountain became known as the Three Sisters."

"Ah, go on," said Chippy with a sceptical eye.
"That's the story I heard many years ago."

*   *   *

Julech took in the silence of the forest, broken from time to time with the harsher sounds of magpies, blue jays and crows and with softer songs of chickadees, wrens, nut hatchers, and juncos. Joining the bird songs were the rat-a-tat-tats of woodpeckers, the flutterings of the grouse and the occasional trill of a grosbeak.

His olfactory nerves were tingling with the smells of spruce, firs, pines, junipers and alders. There were the aromas of fallen acorns, pine needles and rotting logs.

As he walked he reflected on the spiritual insights he had during the past ten days. Three themes kept popping up in his mind: we are created in God's image and likeness; He is the source of all that exists; and, He continues to create through an outpouring of love.

Julech understood his experiences had shaped his image of his God, but that image was miniscule when he tried to imagine the expansiveness of His love. He needed to break through his images of God as a grey bearded old man and just be in His presence. In his limited way, he had felt His presence when he meditated on His love and goodness.

He found it hard to describe God's image as both male and female. When he used the word God or Yahweh, he could imagine God without gender but when he had wanted to use a pronoun, he didn't know what to use. Was it 'He', 'She', 'Him', 'Her,' or 'neither"? He took a simplistic route and referred to his God as both.

As he pondered this further he said to himself, *"Maybe in the grand scheme of things it doesn't matter. We use language to personify the unknowable. We distinguish gender because that is what we know and what defines us in our reality. Maybe that's not how we will be in the next dimension, which some call heaven. In the end, there may be neither male nor female, only an eternal unfolding Love."*

As he hiked he had begun to further understand that the image of God was found in the 'other' and in all of the universe. *He came to realize that this is what is meant by incarnation. The indwelling of God in all.* It didn't matter who or what he related to, he saw reflections of his God.

He thought that when we see the love of God in others, we are moved to respect, love and forgive them. When we see the image of God in the other, we become the hands, feet, eyes and ears of Love. With our hands we lift others up, with our feet we 'walk a mile in their shoes', with our eyes we see the beauty, and with our ears we hear the promptings of this Great Spirit in all of His creation.

When he had regarded the vastness of the universe and drank in the beauty of its unfolding and seemingly unending expansion he could only surmise that a Great Artist must have intended it to become and to have purpose.

As he experienced the mountains, the forests and all of nature around him he soaked in the Artist's creation and asked: "What are we humans doing to it? Why are we treating it with such destructive force? Why are we trying to kill it and everyone and everything in it." He could only come up with one answer, "We want to be God."

"It's Adam and Eve all over again," he shouted.

Julech felt the story of Adam and Eve continued to evolve as it did in days past. The crux of the story was about rejecting God's promptings through pride and self-glorification.

"Are we again denying His promptings and trying to place ourselves above Him and thinking we can take His place?" he wondered. "I see the denials in the movement of those who want to kill all thought about God by claiming there is no God and ridiculing those who believe in Him."

If there is no God, then there is nothing left but to take care of each other. There is nothing higher and nothing more so there is nothing to hope for beyond self. In the end, Julech lamented, this rejection will beget rejection. It will become a black hole of self destruction. Our humanity will revert to our selfish self and our collective and individual false egos will crash down upon us.

"Wake up!" Julech shouted. "It's time to re-connect, to experience the God within us who will make us whole in unity, peace, love, forgiveness and goodness. Wake up! It's time to bury our false egos. Only then can we redeem our world and save it from final destruction."

He concluded that his God of love intended humans to be the antithesis of destroyers. They were to be co-creators who strengthened each other, respected the cosmos and all that it entails, and lived in harmony aligned with His Spirit of love.

*　　*　　*

The sunlight flickered through the forest. All was quiet. Chippy was asleep between his shoulder and pack. Suddenly something flew up in front of them. Its fluttering wings sounded like cannons had gone off in the silent forest.

Julech jumped back, startled. His adrenaline pumped overtime and his heart had kick started into high gear. He was ready to defend himself.

Chippy jumped off and had scurried into the bush.

Within a few seconds Julech realized it was a male spruce grouse. He thought the noise had scared Chippy. He wasn't in sight.

Julech whistled for him.

Chippy didn't return.

Julech whistled again. Still no Chippy.

Julech slid off his pack and sat on a fallen log. He waited for about five minutes, whistled again without a response.

Julech walked over to the area where Chippy had scampered into the bush. Within a short distance he found him. Chippy was feasting on blueberries. He knew something Julech didn't. Spruce grouse liked blueberries.

Julech knew that a male spruce grouse's feathers were gray, black with white spots under his breast and on it's tale. It had a thick bright red patch over each eye. This guy was a male.

Julech wasn't sure whether it had been seeking a mate or whether there was one around. Usually a male spruce grouse would drum, flutter its wings and swish its tail when seeking a mate. He hadn't heard any of that kind of activity.

The spruce grouse had an amazing ability to become immobile and quiet and camouflage itself when it felt threatened. It often allowed predators to come within one or two meters before taking flight. Julech had experienced that behaviour once before when he was hiking with his uncle many years ago. That grouse startled him back then just as this one did earlier.

A spruce grouse eats pine needles, twigs, insects and berries. This was something Chippy knew. Julech thought he ran into the underbrush because he was frightened but soon learned he ran there to see if there were berries. He found blueberry bushes.

Julech joined Chippy and munched on a couple of handfuls of berries and then loaded his last plastic bag with them.

After Chippy had his fill, he crawled up to his navigational post and chipped, "Let's move on!"

Julech got the hint. He put on his pack and they were off.

The forest trail was proving to be an easy walk. The trees formed a canopy and at times he felt he was in nature's cathedral. Light filtered through the spruce and pine trees giving the impression of the cathedral's stained-glass windows. There was no wind, the sky was cloudless and projected a deep blue hue.

His peaceful walk prompted him to continue his reflective review.

*   *   *

Julech discovered that his 'true self' was at rest in his inner core and was intimately connected with a Spirit of Love - a Spirit that prompted him to give of himself to others.

He reasoned that this intimacy found expression in the passion of *Eros* and the passionate self-giving of *Agape*. Both are legitimate and wholesome, and the passion expressed in each is one and the same but expressed differently through his personhood. Both expressed an outpouring of self to others. Both were grounded in humanity and spirituality; and both had deep connections to a spiritual source.

Through *Eros* this Great Spirit of Love was the source of life. He gave breath from His Spiritual Breath. In that way Love continued the re-birthing process. Through *Agape* He continued to spread His unconditional love through us to others.

Julech thought about this and asked himself, "But what holds me in life and why do I continue to exist?"

He concluded that he continued to exist because the spirit which dwelt within him came from an eternal Source that breathed life into all things and held everyone and everything in existence. The closer he came to that spirit, the closer he came to understand his 'true self'.

He came to realize that in this concrete world he is both spirit and body. His physical nature housed his spiritual nature in the same way as his physical nature housed his vital organs. He couldn't live without his vital organs, so too he couldn't live without his spiritual organ, which some call a 'soul'.

He said to himself, "My spiritual organ is the real source of life, and so I need to take care of my spiritual self as I take care of my physical self."

He discovered that *his ultimate quest in life was to find his 'true self' and in this search he could connect with the Spirit of his God.* The two – the 'true self' and the Spirit - welded together as one; and, through the flame of the welding he had to become less while he learned to become more. The fusion of the two *would allow his God of Love to shine through him to others if he could just remain humble in His presence.*

In the quiet of the forest, as one foot crunched before the other and as Chippy lay contented on his shoulder, Julech prayed.

Without You I am nothing, and my true value comes from You. In You I am formed. Without You I am clay. I am formed in the furnace of Love. I have come from You and return to You. You call me by name and keep me warm in the palm of your hands.

Because You formed me, I'm your creation, I can only be my best in You. My life's work is to become the best 'me.' And, to become the best me, I need to lose myself in You - to empty my ego and cling to You in my emptiness, and only then do I find value as I dance with You. Help me become your true partner in our dance.

*　　*　　*

They came upon a meadow with a stream running through it and salted with lily of the valley, yellow blanket and bright red Indian paintbrush flowers. The meadow was lined with a mixture of coniferous trees with low lying willows and juniper shrubs.

Julech recalled his neighbor had produced herbal tea for medicinal purposes from the ripened juniper blue fruit. He thought she would be more than happy to have these buds for her elixir.

Julech decided that this was a good place to stop for lunch. The meadow was a relaxing spot where Julech and Chippy watched butterflies and bees flit from one flower to the other. They ate pieces of biscuit left over from the previous evening, blueberries they picked that morning and the last of the peanut butter balls.

It would have a made a classic picture. Chippy sat on Julech's knee while Julech shared his meal with him. They were communing but not talking. Each in their own world reminiscing about their journey. Each knowing they would soon part, but for now enjoying the meadow and what it had to offer.

Within an hour, Julech stood up and said, "It's time to move on my friend."

Chippy replied, "Let's go."

The valley trail had gradually turned eastward behind Mount Proctor. Julech couldn't see Mount Hosmer but began to feel its presence. The trail continued to wind through the forest and the forest continued to delight Julech's nose with its perfume.

*   *   *

Julech grew in his knowledge of God as love and that everything which exists, exists in that love. This meant for him that everyone should act from the root of love. And, when they acted from that root it produced shoots that bear only the good fruit of compassion, kindness, forgiveness, humility and joy. *Love became what love generated* as he explored, albeit in a different way, during his discussions with George and Jen.

This realization of God's love didn't make him worthier than others. *Everyone is held with the same boundless and all forgiving love. As such he too must extend his love to others regardless of how they act and he must dare to forgive them.*

He came to understand that this is what Jesus meant when he asked Christians to love their enemies, turn the other cheek, and forgive them for they didn't know what they were doing (Mt:5:39-43; Lk:23:34). Jesus loved those who persecuted Him. He pointed out their errors and still loved them.

Julech felt that this love within Love gave people hope and courage to go to their hurting places. Not that the Spirit of Love removed their hurt, but that the Spirit would sustain them in their hurt. Love somehow took away the feelings of pain, sadness, and loneliness and replaced them with a modicum of painlessness, joy and aliveness, not in some magical fashion but in Love's mystical sustaining embrace as it did when he remembered Noella.

He solidified his earlier musings about life's journey and finding one's true self. It was all about coming to an understanding of God's love and fusing with this Love. And, when he entered this fusion or communion he began to shed what was 'not good' and what 'took him away from goodness'. It encouraged him to turn *FROM* discontent, negativity, destruction, immorality, selfishness and ego glorification, *TOWARD* compassion, forgiveness, mercy, non-violence, justice, respect, inclusiveness, and oneness. And in the process of this turning *he learned that everyone was inherently godly, intrinsically lovable and fully dignified.*

Everyday during his hike Julech discovered that his God was with him through the indwelling of His Spirit. He was not up there or down there. He was with him in the moment and whenever he extended himself to others by bringing them comfort, solace and hope.

He was with Julech in the beauty of the sunrises and sunsets, the rains, rainbows, the animals and birds, and the dancing stars at night. *Julech saw Him not with his physical eye but with his inner eye.*

He knew that his physical eye brought in the beauty of the outside, and he learned that he could only see that beauty with his inner eye. When he reflected on what he had seen, even when it wasn't there he could still revel in the beauty image presented to him, just as he was now reflecting on the memories of the beauty he saw during the past days.

He said to himself, "*We see with our physical eye, but we only see the fullness of God's creation and goodness with our inner eye, even in the least of things such as dirt and a worm.*"

This seeing he concluded can only come about when we bury the projections of our false ego, and all that it contains and retains - our machinations, rituals, theology, philosophy and what we believe we know and feel. Only when we humbly stare inwardly could we become one with the Holy and touch the glimmers of His love. And, in the touching we are challenged to reach out to those He loved most deeply the vulnerable, marginalized, exploited, limited, disregarded, different, and any other exclusionary term humans appropriate to people not like them.

Julech sought God and had found that He was with him all along.

He began to understand the bearded man's wisdom. God was intrinsically bound within him, if he but listened. He is hidden but not hidden outside him, if he but looked.

*   *   *

As Julech was listening to his God speak to him in the forest, Chippy remained silent at his navigational post until he saw someone approaching. It was a hiker with a staff and a beard. Chippy didn't move but thumped on Julech's head. Julech was taken aback. He appeared similar to the fellow he met on the first day of his hike. Julech stopped and waited for him to draw near.

"Hi," Julech greeted the man. "You sure seem familiar. Have we met before?"

"Maybe," the man offered. "What have you discovered so far?"

Before Julech could reply the man walked past him. He was in a hurry.

The hiker looked back, "I understand your journey has allowed you to look and listen deeper. Keep doing so. By the way there's a lake about an hour up the trail. It has fish in it.

A great place to break bread and rest for the night. You should be home by early afternoon."

This short encounter shook Julech as he had just thought about him a few minutes earlier. He sat down and refreshed himself with water.

"Who the heck is that guy?"

Chippy bent over from his perch and checked Julech's eyes. He could see the bewilderment in them but for Chippy there wasn't any bewilderment.

He chipped, "Please give me a few nuts and water and then let's move on to the lake. Our day isn't done yet."

*　　*　　*

Julech was still puzzled as to who the man was but he heeded Chippy's request. The lake sounded like a good place to stop for the night.

Indeed, the day wasn't done yet and that reminded him about his musing regarding God's timelessness and humanities timeliness.

He knew that humans had invented time as linear and measured it in nano seconds, seconds, minutes, hours, days, weeks, months, and years. In his discussions he could go back in time and talk about the future. He unfolded in time, and the world unfolded in the same time. He was inside of time, limited and bound. But, he conjectured, God didn't view time in that way. He was in another dimension.

Julech tried to wrap his head around that concept and he could only come up with, "God viewed time from above so to speak where as he experienced time from below."

His God was omnipresent – in the moment. He had no beginning and no end. He was, is and will be all at once. He is "I AM,

Who AM," YHWH." He had no limits. He was fullness, a totality outside of time.

To live in the omnipresence of God was to live not for tomorrow, not for yesterday but for the moment.

God was with him, was within him and when he encountered Him in silence, in others and in the beauty of all that existed, he encountered the Holy. His presence engendered peace and joy.

Julech thought about these things in this way:

I encounter Him inside time but outside of time. I find Him in silence. I meet Him not in ritual, a building, by someone else's saying or even in the forest and the mountains. These are but the reflections of His love and beauty. As I gaze on those reflections, I meet Him in the moment. In those times without time, God rest's in me and I in Him. In those moments I am accepted through His forgiveness, I am embraced through His love, and I am moved to act in His name to be forgiving, compassionate, patient, kind and gentle.

To live in the moment, I must get out of the moment. I need to see things from a different perspective - God's perspective, the wholeness of time in eternity. When I lose myself in the timeless now and not worry about the little things that disturb me I become free to spend a moment with my God. And if I can string those moments together everything I see, hear, touch, smell or do becomes important as they are driven by the Spirit of Love. To truly live in such moments, I can only reflect His love. I look in the mirror, so to speak, and see His Love returning to me and through me to others. If I live with this realization I can only do good for others and thus be His beacon in this world.

*   *   *

Julech had been hiking directly east at the base of Mount Hosmer when he happened upon the lake the stranger mentioned. It wasn't large but there was a creek flowing in at the headwaters and another flowing out at the mouth. It was nestled between Mount Proctor and Mount Hosmer and surrounded by pine and spruce trees. There was a clearing on the south side and lodge poles sticking out on the north side. The clearing had several fire pit markings ringed with rocks and small stacks of wood. No doubt this was a spot where campers came to fish and search for wild berries. It might also have been a starting point for hikers to walk the Black Gold Trail.

Chippy was interested in testing the nearby area for berries, nuts and insects. Julech was interested in testing the waters with fly fishing. A couple of brook trout would suit him just fine for his final meal on the trail.

The fish weren't interested in catching flies that evening, so Julech switched to grub. He dug up a couple of worms, placed them on the hook and threw his line into the water. That's what the fish wanted. In no time he had a couple of trout and was ready to fry them.

Chippy found what he was looking for as well. He by-passed the squirming insects and discovered wild raspberries.

Julech searched his bag to see what he had left to complement the fish. He found the bag of blueberries he picked earlier that day, a small bag of dried vegetables with rice, and a few nuts. Fish, blueberries and rice with vegetables sounded like a good meal. He laid out the remaining nuts and blueberries for Chippy.

Once the meal was prepared he whistled for Chippy. They sat there in the quiet of the evening and supped together. As it turned to dusk, Julech searched the face of Mount Hosmer and said to Chippy, "See that shadow in the middle of the mountain."

Chippy stood up and gazed at the mountain. Somehow, he sensed that there was a story coming from Julech.

> There is an old legend, Julech explained, that in 1887 William Fernie was combing the Crowsnest Mountains prospecting for minerals. He and his fellow prospectors came across a First Nations group of people. He noticed an Indian Princess wearing a beautiful necklace of polished coal. He wanted to know where she got the coal, so he began a romantic relationship with her. Unfortunately, after she revealed the source of the coal Fernie left her to lay his claim. She was heartbroken by his lack of trustworthiness and asked her father, the Chief, to place a curse on him and the valley. Over time, the curse plagued the valley and Fernie BC experienced two devastating fires, major flooding and numerous mining disasters.

> As a visible symbol of the curse, a shadow, called the Ghost Rider, appears on the face of Mount Hosmer from spring through fall. The shadow clearly shows the Princess riding on a horse with the Chief walking beside her, leading the horse.

"Now I know why you called the trail we hiked the 'Black Gold'," chipped Chippy.

"You got it," Julech smiled.

"Does Fernie still have the curse?"

"No, the curse was lifted in 1964. Members of the Kootenai Tribe led by Chief Red Eagle, gathered in Fernie for a ceremonial lifting of the curse.

"Good."

The sun set. Julech watched the fire burn down while he sipped his coffee. He realized he had lost track of the time that day. He had been mesmerized by the walk through the enchanted forest while engrossed in his thoughts, musings and meditations. He was now ready to call it a day. Tomorrow he would be back with his Catrela. He had a delightful hiking experience, but he couldn't wait to get home and be with her.

And so, ended the eleventh day.

Going Home

LOUD ECHOING BUGLE CALLS PIERCED THE MORNING AIR. CHIPPY opened one eye and knew it was one of nature's calls often heard in the dawning of the day. Julech sat straight up and looked around.

"What the heck was that?"

There, across the lake among the lodgepoles was a bull elk in the prime of life. His antlers had five tines each and he was looking squarely at Julech.

It was near the end of July and mating season was fast approaching.

"Was this elegant specimen testing his vocals to attract a female, and not necessarily to wake me up?" he asked the Chip.

"Yah, sure," Chippy demurred.

Julech learned from his nature studies that elk had graced this land for millions of years, weighed-in up to 240 kilograms, had four-chambered stomachs and ate up to 7 kilograms of vegetation daily. He also knew that elk could swim.

Julech didn't need to concern himself about that as the animal pulled himself out of the water and disappeared among the trees.

"What a way to start the last day of our hike. We're being called to attention by a bugle call at the break of day."

He almost felt that he should hoist a flag and give a morning salute.

*　　*　　*

That bugle call and the impression of elk gracing the land for millions of years triggered another meditative notion reminiscent of his time on the trail.

From the beginning of time God continues to create. He is always near, calling forth his unfolding love and grace so that we may have life in full abundance.

Whatever we do, whatever activity we participate in, whatever work we take on, we participate in this great unfolding. There isn't separation between our activity and the spirit - our activity and spirit of love are one. Our participation in God's love infused our activity, and our activity expresses God's love through Christ in the world. Through faith and hope we become clothed in the love of Christ and merge with Him. In this way we become the hands of Christ.

This brings new meaning to our activity and our work. It raises what we do to a whole new level so that what we do, no matter how low the task, we are able to do it in the spirit of love and in that way, we participate in the transforming nature of God's love.

*This doesn't make our work or activity any easier,
but it does give it a renewed purpose. This love-spirit
pushes us to do our best in whatever we do and
inspires us to do more to strengthen communities
by seeking justice, compassion and peace for all.*

Julech focused on one of the wild flowers and realized his limited knowledge of God was like a flower. The seed contained all that was known about the flower and only in time as the flower unfolded did he begin to see and appreciate its beauty. So too as he evolved, his understanding of God unveiled itself. It was deepened through the wisdom he had gained from the past and would come to full fruition as he stepped into the future.

*We only know God from what is known, and what we
don't know is yet to be revealed in time. We are all on
the road to this knowing and we need to be open to
His promptings that come to us from all of creation
and a truth that is found in all insights, philosophies,
sciences and religions - a wisdom that ties all of us
together as one in Him.*

Julech bowed down, looked at Chippy and said, "I still have much to learn."

Chippy looked up and chipped, "I'm alright with your unfolding God."

As Julech was ending his reflections he questioned whether there was a straight path to knowing his God. A straight stairway allowing him to see Him step by step. At one time he thought so, and logically he tried to define the undefinable. *He now realized that his journey to the unknown God was more of an evolutionary process, filled with surprises and slippery slopes as he spiraled toward Love's everlasting embrace.*

Maranatha, he chanted.

*   *   *

Julech got up emptied his pack and found one serving of rolled oats, a bit of dried fruit, and two energy bars. His stash of food had diminished. It was time to take the last steps of his journey home. He put out some oats and dried fruit for Chippy, but Chippy had disappeared. He had gone to the raspberry patch and chipped madly for Julech to come.

"Aha!" Julech exclaimed. "Now I know where you were last evening. Thanks for letting me know."

He bent down and picked a bag of raspberries for the two of them.

After breakfast and his last cup of coffee, Julech doused the fire, looked at the serenity of the lake and said to Chippy, "Let's go."

"I'm with you," he chipped.

The coniferous forest of evergreens gave way to a variety of deciduous trees. Julech and Chippy hiked among birch, aspen, maple and towering cottonwood trees. Every once and a while he came across a chokecherry and crab apple tree hidden away just off the trail. He was now traversing straight east and expected to do so until noon.

*   *   *

Julech's mind turned to how the Spirit of Love continues to prompt us, and, in the process, we find Him.

> *He felt a welling up inside of him that said, "Our union with God is life saving, soul saving and love saving." He can only love us. He is there with His love even when we reject Him. He is the Hound of Heaven as Francis Thompson expresses in the poem of the same name.*

He chases us with His love. We only need to realize He is there, waiting for us to join Him. He is within us and we in Him. Even when we reject Him, He is still there waiting for us. We can't escape.

We lift ourselves up in praise and bow down in worship, not because all things are God, but because in and through them we find His Spirit.

Julech concluded that we couldn't know God as an object of teaching. We could only be with Him in relationship through love and acceptance. Hence to try to rationalize God was futile - it became a theological or theoretical proposition. God could not be objectified. He could only come to us in faith, love and hope.

He prompts us everywhere and anywhere if we open ourselves to hear His call. He whispers to us in the noise of thunder and the quiet of the rain, the artist's renderings, the music of song, orchestra and jazz, the cry of the poor, the cacophony of the street, the fun and laughter of children, the relationship with the other, and the quietude of silence. All we need to do is be open to His call and listen to His voice.

Julech also learned that as this Great Love seeks us we could seek Him. All we had to do was knock on His door and He would open it (Matt. 7:7). How could we find Him or be in His presence if we didn't look, knock and be open for Him to speak with us? *He is always present, waiting for us to call on Him.*
In the quiet of his hike Julech went deep within himself.

I am weak. He prompts me to turn away from selfishness and turn to His love. I reject His promptings. He still loves and prompts. He lets me express my freedom in my rejection but still remains at my side.

My selfishness is more important to me than listening to His promptings. Acquiesce, and I will know His peace, grace, and love. Reject, and I will continue to stroke my false ego and be at war within myself. He waits patiently for my turning away from my false self and turning to Him within my true self.

He prompts. He Loves. He holds me in the palm of His hands. I know this. I believe this. Yet in my frailty I turn away from Him. I must turn to Him. His Spirit will give my spirit strength. Yet, He will not intervene. He respects my freedom to turn to Him or to turn away from Him.

He waits. He loves. He wants me to love Him in return. He even calls me by my name (Is 43:1) He wants me as a partner in His love. It's up to me to reject my selfishness and my darker promptings. He will give me strength, grace and be at my side, but I must call on Him. I must knock on his door. He is waiting to hear my knock with more love than I can imagine.

Julech prayed.

Hear my knock! Help me in my yearning for You. Help me to reject my selfishness and bury my false ego. Help me to accept Your love, Your promptings and Your grace with humility.

*   *   *

It was near noon and a good time to break for lunch. He and Chippy had made good time that morning and he expected to arrive at the bridge around three in the afternoon.

Chippy jumped from the *Chapeau* and quickly ran into the underbrush. He had heard something special there. Julech didn't pay any heed as Chippy had always wanted to run after a long hiking stretch.

Julech went into the trees to relieve himself and there he saw a mighty oak tree with acorn droppings scattered all around it.

"What a find and what a surprise I will have for Chippy when he returns."

He filled half of his pack with the golden acorns.

He returned to the trail and the small opening where they had stopped, and he whistled for Chippy. Chippy didn't respond. Again, Julech wasn't concerned because he discovered during the hike that Chippy had a knack of finding goodies under bushes. When he was ready he would respond to the whistle.

Julech munched on his last energy bar, raspberries and a piece of cheese. He remained still to listen to the song birds, rustling of leaves and the whooshing of the tall grass. He sat there for a long time and waited for Chippy.

He whistled several times and still Chippy didn't return. Now, Julech was concerned so he walked into the bush and whistled some more.

No response.

He walked further.

A loud chipmunkese shout greeted him.

There high up on a birch tree was Chippy.

Chippy looked down at Julech, winked, flicked his tail wildly and thumped loudly. Julech could hear him say, "I'm alright with God and so are you. We've had a great time together but now we must part. You go your way and I'll go mine."

Chippy had found a mate. He wasn't going to join Julech to the end of his journey home. After all, Julech was going home to

Catrela so why not make a new home in this neck of the woods with Chipella.

Julech experienced a mix of emotions but he understood. He went to the bottom of the birch tree and emptied the acorns and the remaining berries he had in his pack. He looked up the birch tree one more time and tipped his *Chapeau*, turned and joined the trail home.

*   *   *

Julech trekked to the trail bordering the highway. He was travelling southward to Ferris Creek where Catrela would meet him. On this section of the trail he reopened one more unexpected gift he had received during his journey of self-discovery – *the freedom he found when he realized he was and is consumed in an all-embracing love.*

Julech mused that often humans had tried to gift wrap God. They put Him in a box and attempted to tie a ribbon around it. In so doing they confined Him and claimed him as 'ours' to the exclusion of others. Julech was certain that God couldn't be boxed. He was too big. He was beyond boxing. Whenever people tried to box Him they became narrow in their approach toward Him and toward each other. They became exclusionary, divisive, protective and constrictive.

> *God is the great unpacking and unboxing. He is our unrestricted and unexpected gift, freely given and outside of any constraint. We accept Him as IS, as Being, as constant flow of Love without beginning and without end. How can that be boxed, contained or controlled?*
>
> *Unpack and unbox God and He will unpack and unbox us.*

When we place this Great Spirit outside the box, we become inclusive, accepting, humble, forgiving, loving and giving. He will set us free in His Spirit and within that freedom there is no room for divisiveness, wars, violence, rancour, or anger - only peace, acceptance and service in love.

Julech's journey had taught him about the unboxing of God's gift freely given: that he was created from Love's eternal unfolding; that his purpose was to serve all that existed with love; and, that at the end of his life's journey he would return to everlasting Love.

Now he must take the lessons he learned from those twelve days and turn them into action.

*   *   *

Julech was getting close to Ferris Creek.

He could hardly contain his excitement.

He arrived at the bridge, a bit dishevelled and bearded.

The SUV pulled up.

Catrela stepped out in her garden clothes.

They looked at each other with deep affection, hesitantly touched and then fully embraced as if for the first time.

Catrela stepped into the SUV. Julech followed. They drove home in silence, overwhelmed with each other's presence, yet eager to hear the other's stories of the past twelve days.

Acknowledgements

I owe a huge thank you to those who willingly took the time to read, comment and converse with me about the original manuscript of *Eternal Unfolding*. To Joan Morin, John Meehan SJ, Anne Campbell, and my dear friends who attend our monthly coffee group: Margaret Herman, Don McGuire, Fr. Joe Firkola, and Emil Kutarna. Your wisdom, keen insight and suggestions were invaluable. (On October 23,2018, Father Joe was wrapped in the arms of Eternal Love. He will be dearly missed by all those who knew him.)

To Carolyn and our two daughters Treena and Leanne goes my deep appreciation for your encouragement, comments and editing notes. A special thank you to Carolyn, for her patience and giving me the space to think, write and toil away on *Eternal Unfolding*.

To Dale Swanston for the photo included on the Title Page, depicting a panoramic view looking northward from Lizard Range and the inspiration for the opening paragraphs of *Eternal Unfolding*.

To all those at Tellwell Publishing: Scott Lunn, my first contact with Tellwell Publishing who convinced me to test out what Tellwell has to offer; Elliot Hockley, my Project Manager, who ably guided me through the publishing steps; Vanessa, who gave a valuable evaluation of the original manuscript; Bonnie who designed the cover and interior layout; and, all those who assisted with the design and publishing of the finished product.

And, to all those who encouraged me to write a book about matters pertaining to the Spirit. Thank you!

About the Author

Richard P. Fontanie was born and spent his youth in Fernie BC. He is married, has two married daughters and three grandchildren. He has an MSW and worked for 18 years as a senior and executive public servant. In 1984 he founded Fontanie Associates Consulting Services Inc., a management consulting and training firm. One of his guiding principles has always been to help others find their true selves and become the best they can be in all aspects of their lives. He now spends his time mentoring and coaching executives and senior managers; and, writing articles based on his years of experience as an executive, business owner, facilitator, consultant, and coach. If so inclined, you can read his blogs and articles at www.fontaniemagazine.com. *Eternal Unfolding* is his first novel.

Find More on The Net

FERNIE, BC

Fernie:

tourismfernie.com/activities

Heiko Trail:

https://fernie.com/blog/2012/09/
mountain-lakes-trail-into-your-heart/

Three Sister Mountain:

www.summitpost.org/three-sisters/426755

Bisaro Cave:

http://calgaryherald.com/technology/science/
calgary-explorers-help-uncover-canadas-deepest-cave

Giant Ammonites:

https://fernie.com/blog/2010/11/another-giant-ammonite/

Westminster Abbey

Westminster Abbey:

www.westminsterabbey.ca/

Reminiscent of The Abbey mentioned in the story.

POEMS

Theresa of Avila poem

www.journeywithjesus.net/PoemsAndPrayers/Teresa_Of_Avila_Christ_Has_No_Body.shtml

St Francis of Assisi Brother Sun and Sister Moon song:

www.catholic.org/prayers/prayer.php?p=183

Robert Frost, The Road Not Taken

www.poets.org/poetsorg/poem/road-not-taken

Francis Thompson, Hound of Heaven,

http://www.bartleby.com/236/239.html

Sam Walter Foss, The Calf Path

www.poets.org/poetsorg/poem/calf-path

MEDITATION

Christian Meditation Method:

http://wccm.org/

or https://pray-as-you-go.org/home/

Reflective and Contemplative Meditations:

https://cac.org/

Centering Prayer:
www.contemplativeoutreach.org/

category/category/centering-prayer

Dr. Wayne Dyer: Getting in the Gap video

www.youtube.com/watch?v=KADc4U2rng0

PEOPLE

Pope Francis

https://en.wikipedia.org/wiki/Pope_Francis

Mother Teresa

https://en.wikipedia.org/wiki/Mother_Teresa

Corrie ten Boom

https://en.wikipedia.org/wiki/Corrie_ten_Boom

Teresa of Avila

https://en.wikipedia.org/wiki/Teresa_of_Ávila

Francis of Assisi

https://en.wikipedia.org/wiki/Francis_of_Assisi

ANIMALS AND BIRDS

Learn more about the animals and birds identified in this book at Wikipedia

Read more by Richard Fontanie:

www.Fontaniemagazine.com

www.ingramcontent.com/pod-product-compliance
Lightning Source LLC
LaVergne TN
LVHW090626160726
843309LV00011B/456